To Ling – gone but never forgotten.
Every time the sky looks magical – like the neons of
an orange sunset, or a giant glowing moon – I think of you.

this book belongs to

o o o o o o o o o o o o o o o o o o o o o o o o o o o o o o o o o o o

OPEN

A TOOLKIT FOR HOW MAGIC AND MESSED UP LIFE CAN BE

Gemma Cairney

Illustrated by
Aurelia Lange

MACMILLAN

First published 2017 by Macmillan Children's Books
an imprint of Pan Macmillan
20 New Wharf Road, London N1 9RR
Associated companies throughout the world
www.panmacmillan.com

ISBN 978-1-5098-3611-6

Designed by Janene Spencer
Printed and bound in China

CONTENTS

I am brave
I am brash
I am bold
I am wild
I love to cuddle
I am loud . . . but
I am vulnerable
I love to smooch
I am serene
I am bored
BUT ALWAYS EXCITED
I am goofy
I am beautiful
Why do I find it so hard to write that?
I am deeply saddened
but at the same time so happy
I LOVE my life and I love the world
I sometimes don't like myself though
I am not perfect
I'm sometimes tired
I am always raring to go

I am as deep as an old well
I am shallow like a lame puddle
I am strange
which means I am normal
I am not preaching
I am a friend
with an OPEN heart

I am me.

WELCOME

Welcome to *Open: A Toolkit for How Magic and Messed Up Life Can Be*.

This book is here to be your guide in times of need. Keep it on your shelf and go to specific chapters during those moments in life that mess with your head, or leaf through and devour it cover to cover. By opening this book you have become part of #TeamOpen, and part of the movement for open hearts and minds. There is no one that this book isn't for.

During years of presenting, and more recently with *The Surgery* on Radio 1, I've encountered a huge variety of people who are dealing with lots of different things in their own ways. My own life hasn't always been easy, and whilst I've dealt with some of the stuff that comes up in this book, I'm not an expert in everything – all I can do is communicate openly about what I've been through and be a friend. I've consulted lots of people who are experts in the issues covered, though – along with a list of people and organizations to speak to if you need more information on anything.

This book covers some tough stuff, but there's nothing you wouldn't find in the storyline of a popular soap opera, and definitely NOTHING you wouldn't find within a four-second Google search. *Open* is about real life and everything that comes with it.

This book isn't all about me, it's also about you and all the other incredibly clever, brutally honest, brave and awesomely inspiring voices woven within its pages. This book is yours and I want you to personalize it in any way you see fit; to embellish it and make your own mark on the pages. There are no rules. Douse it in gorgeous gold pen, doodle across it with a blunt pencil or a defiant marker pen, or cover it in magical stickers – and whatever your approach, feel free to respond to however the words make you feel.

Just  YOU

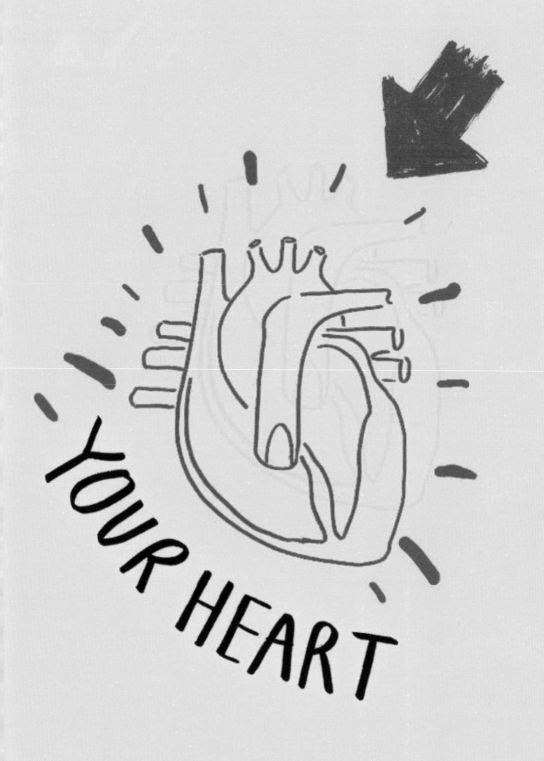

YOUR HEART

YOUR HEART is precious. It is AWESOME. Not only does it pump blood around your body to keep you alive, but it is the root of your deepest emotions.

YOUR HEART is your Emotional Mothership, your inner hub – the place where you feel joy, happiness, anger, fear, sadness, heartbreak, confusion – a cosmic, blinding mass of feelings that can sometimes feel overwhelming but make you the unique and incredible human being that you are.

YOUR HEART is tough – it is a warrior – it will heal you and bring you joy as much as it will cause you to hurt and even to physically ache sometimes. Right now I'm taking you on a journey through your heart, through the people and situations that touch your heart, that bump it along the way, that soothe it and that make it want to burst with emotions.

REMEMBER that at the centre of your heart is a wonderful, scary, intangible and dizzyingly powerful thing called **LOVE**.

Love is your greatest ally. Whether it is for people, music, plants – or a goldfish, **LOVE ALWAYS WINS.**

4

FAMILY

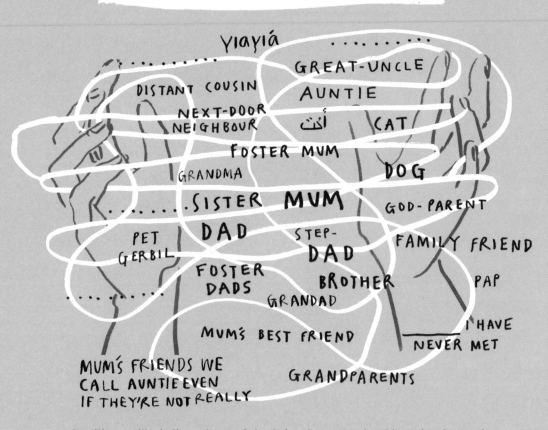

yιαyιά

GREAT-UNCLE

DISTANT COUSIN

AUNTIE

NEXT-DOOR
NEIGHBOUR   أَبْت   CAT

FOSTER MUM

GRANDMA   DOG

SISTER MUM   GOD-PARENT

PET   DAD   STEP-   FAMILY FRIEND
GERBIL   DAD

FOSTER   BROTHER   PAP
DADS   GRANDAD

                                I HAVE
MUM'S BEST FRIEND   NEVER MET

MUM'S FRIENDS WE
CALL AUNTIE EVEN   GRANDPARENTS
IF THEY'RE NOT REALLY

Families are like balls made up of elastic bands, wrapped and bound and wound around each other, linked by similarities and connections. We are linked to others, but individuals too. The truth is that families aren't perfect, ever. More often than not, families are far from 'conventional'. But these peeps, the ones who brought us into the world, help form who we are and who we will go on to be.

Remember there is no such thing as a 'normal' family.

Let's kick off with PARENTS. When it comes to parents, we love to label them, don't we? There are step-parents, divorced parents, single parents, adopted parents, foster parents, estranged parents, good parents, bad parents, boring parents, uptight parents, possessive parents, depressed parents, parents that argue, so-in-love-it-grosses-us-out-cos-we-hear-them-having-sex-sometimes parents, parents-we-never-see-for-some-reason-like-'they-are-always-at-work' parents, parents who are hard to please, parents who have passed away, parents we miss so much it makes our eyes sting at the thought of them.

Then there are those beings (more like aliens) we call siblings: BROTHERS and SISTERS. When it comes to brothers and sisters, the labels and emotive descriptions come thick and fast out of the box again: step-siblings, siblings you get on really well with, siblings you hate, siblings you envy, competitive siblings, siblings you have nothing to say to, siblings you've never met, half-brothers or half-sisters.

Or of course you might be an ONLY CHILD, or maybe you feel like an only child because your sibling or siblings are a lot older or younger than you and you didn't grow up with them.

IT'S COMPLICATED...

Hand in the air if you can identify with one or more of these families? Millions of us have higgledy-piggledy, eclectic family trees. Some of us have detailed horror stories and fabulous family-specific tales that drip from the leaves too. I do, and so do most of the people I know. Even if we find our personal family patchwork generally OK, at some point EVERYONE FINDS THEIR FAMILY EMBARRASSING. No one – and I repeat NO ONE – escapes that.

chatting to your 'rents

When the poo hits the fan, hopefully you can talk to your mum or dad, or your foster parent, or your guardian – whoever looks after you – about your worries and fears. If you don't feel like you have someone who fits that description, then find someone who is older than you, wiser than you, that you trust and who gives good advice. Even if that person is on the end of a phone. These people do exist, I promise. A teacher, a doctor or someone from a qualified organization or support network – if life is getting tough, they'll help you start to figure out what is puzzling you or bringing you down. Even if they can't perform perfect wizardry and magic answers out of the air, they will be able to point you in the right direction.

A problem shared can be a problem halved.

College/university

Research what help is available to you here, even if you're not feeling like you need help right now – it's good to know that it's there for you. Most colleges and universities provide free and confidential in-house counselling services, with professionally qualified counsellors and access to specific external advice.

Teacher/school

Schools are set up and ready to hear from their students, whether it's about exam pressure or problems at home.

Your Workplace

Many companies have an HR department. The HR stands for Human Resources and is designed to protect the well-being of the employee, especially if it is an issue relating to the workplace itself. Some HR departments are better than others (they aren't always the answer). But it's worth researching yours specifically and knowing your rights within your place of work. Ask around and work out what's in place to protect and look after you.

A mate's mum

Sometimes borrowing someone else's mum is pretty helpful. They can offer an unbiased perspective as well as having the mum qualities you need.

Your GP/doctor

If you break your arm, you go to the doctor. If you are feeling stressed, anxious and filled with heartache because of it, your doctor may be able to help with this too.

When your parents are being hot-headed monsters and saying no to something . . .

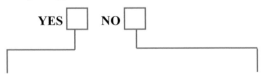

When you feel that parents are acting all unapproachable and saying no to something you want to do, remember that most of them instinctively want to protect you, feed you and get you educated and equipped. They want to prepare you for the big wide world. They literally can't help it. Imagine if you could see your face in someone smaller than you, and that you've been through life's highs and lows, and all you want more than anything in the whole wide world is for the face of the person smaller than you to be smiling and oozing joy. You'd WRESTLE A DINOSAUR to protect them.

Even though families can make us roar like no other and prod our emotional pressure points in a way that only they can, I want you to know that your family is only doing its job, which is to make you generally feel loved and safe. If you are reading this with a family member nearby, go give them a cuddle. Or do it next time you see them. Then answer this:

Did it make you glow and feel warm inside?

YES ☐   NO ☐

If the answer is YES to feeling warm and glowing from the inside from hugging at least one of your family members, then this a good sign – remember this next time you feel like they are against you!

If the answer is NO and you are not getting on with any of your family, you are lacking their presence in any way, you feel truly alone or in your gut you are very uncomfortable with something that's going on in your family at the moment – please read on.

DYSFUNCTIONAL FAMILIES

There is a difference between a MESSY family and a family that makes you feel unsafe or uncared for. Hopefully you have someone in your family who is strong and looks out for you – but issues such as alcoholism, addiction, depression, divorce, money worries or unemployment can rock your parents and make it difficult for them to cope. Please remember it is not your job to take on their problems, but there are people you can talk to about how to cope with your own feelings.

Please ask yourself these three things:

1) **Is it affecting your everyday life?** ☐

2) **Are you scared in any way?** ☐

3) **Would you like some extra help with this situation?** ☐

If you ticked any of the above, please tell someone in authority that you are feeling this way and why. I REPEAT: speak to a teacher, or your GP, if that seems more appropriate, or head to the back of this book for a list of organizations that are expert in helping with specific issues, no matter how hard or scary they seem. You are NOT alone.

Who's your Daddy?

From the age of seven, like many kids I knew, I grew up in a single-parent household. It was my mum who brought me and my sister up, though we'd see our dad regularly – a man I wholly adore.

My dad is a gentle, lovely, sweet, friendly man – he moved to the UK from Jamaica when he was eight, and his face is the kindest I've ever seen. In the late 1970s he used to be the guitarist in a band called the High Flames, a fact I will never not find brilliantly glamorous. He still plays guitar, and can copy any tune from an advert and transform it into funk. His favourite band is Earth, Wind & Fire – one of the grooviest bands your ears could hear.

On my dad's fiftieth birthday it seemed like the whole of his estate came to the birthday barbecue, because everyone loves him. They practically lined up to tell me how cool they thought he was. The grannies enthused about how they could moan till they were blue in the face to him and he would always listen, how they loved that he'd still go to church every Sunday and genuinely cared if they were OK. Even the naughtiest-of-naughty bad boys on the estate loved him. I think it's because he never judges, he cares passionately about social justice, thinks anything is possible, and his resting face is the warmest smile! If the sun had a face, it'd smile like my dad's. He always looks cool too – ironed short-sleeved shirt, slick, gelled curls, sparklingly clean sunglasses and a heavy, dependable watch. He's a hero. He and my mum didn't work out, but that's their stuff. I'm eternally lucky to have him in my life.

One of the most amazing things about my dad is that he is not my 'biological' dad, my 'real' dad. I never knew my real dad (I don't like that phrase, 'real dad' – it doesn't describe what feels 'real' to me in relation to how I feel about either of my dads. The most I knew about my biological dad – my BD – is that he was a wildly charismatic, deep-voiced firework of a man, who had a gold tooth. He had Jamaican parents too, was from the Midlands, loved to party, was sometimes violent and was an alcoholic.

When I was nineteen, I got a letter from the Samaritans, who informed me that they'd had an enquiry from a distant family member of mine who would like to get in touch. I knew instantly it would have something to do with this other dad of mine, floating out there somewhere. A dad for whom I'd never felt the need, because I already had one, who was the grooviest, smiliest, funniest dad of all dads.

Out of intrigue, I agreed to be put in contact with whoever it was that had enquired. It turned out to be the sister of my BD – an aunt I'd never met – and she wanted to tell me that he'd died. I'd never known this man, but a spiral of mashed feelings washed over me, as if someone had turned out the lights and put on a continuous flickering strobe instead. It didn't feel like direct and identifiable grief – it felt more like when you hear about someone dying that you may have only met once. It made me sad, but it didn't make me want to fall to the ground and smash everything up. I hadn't seen this man since I was three – he hadn't been part of my life. I didn't know what I felt. I almost couldn't feel.

Around this time, I met with my 'real' grandparents – one of the most startling experiences of my life, seeing my own face in these two people's faces. It was frankly insane. But then I decided to move on. I got on with my early twenties, carried on disco-dancing, smooching hotness and chasing dreams. But grief got to me all the same. Even though I didn't recognize it. It began gnawing at my insides, sometimes in the form of a searing pain in my chest. It was a longing for answers, a buried anxiety about the alcoholism that had killed this stranger who was my dad. My feelings were chewed up – sometimes making me self-destructive.

Eventually I worked through these feelings and threw myself into life, with the one thing that I was wholly sure of strapped to my back: that I LOVE LIFE. But what I learned was that grief – especially when it's for family – can flip open your heart, and out come unexpected messy feelings and pain you aren't prepared for. I realized that even though he wasn't around for me, my BD is still part of me, part of my identity, and I tortured myself thinking about his drinking, wondering if anyone could have stopped him. But his addiction wasn't my fault – I had to learn that. Even though it affected me more than I realized.

I worked on my 'happy' – surrounded myself with things and people that made me glow inside. Dug deep to face up to the sad and confusing stuff in my heart and turn it into energy – to charge forward and be brave.

And now? Now I don't question what I should feel about either of my Jamaican dads: my BD, who I never knew and whose face I've inherited, and the one who is still here for me, whose face is like the sunshine and the kindest and most dignified man I've been lucky enough to know. I feel OK. I love and am proud to have my heart beating to a reggae rhythm, and to have a soul that now understands how complicated families can be.

Everyone has a family tale to tell.

Lauren, from Garmouth, Scotland

Lauren's mum and dad split up when she was six. After that, she says, her dad 'gradually lost touch' with her and her sister. Her mum has since remarried, and her stepdad has adopted her. Lauren says, 'Last time I spoke to my biological dad, he was working for Virgin trains – so every time I use one I wonder if he's driving.'

Michael, from Scarborough

'I have three mums and three dads – the perks of being adopted and having step-parents also. I'm in contact with every single one of them too. My mum and dad will always be my parents, but I'm grateful to my birth mum, for her sacrifice to give me the best possible upbringing.'

Sophie, from Sussex

'Having a gay dad and a gay brother is something I am so proud of. It represents the diversity and acceptance in my family; it demonstrates an unconditional love we all have for each other; but most of all it makes me happy that they are content to be themselves. It is very special and is at the heart of what makes my unconventional family truly awesome.'

FAMILY BINGO

Roll up, roll up. Who's for a game of FAMILY BINGO?
Simply fill in the blanks: write the thing you most like
and dislike about all the flavours of your family.

Name: Good: Bad:	Name: Good: Bad:	Name: Good: Bad:	Name: Good: Bad:	Name: Good: Bad:
Name: Good: Bad:	Name: Good: Bad:	Name: Good: Bad:	Name: Good: Bad:	Name: Good: Bad:
Name: Good: Bad:	Name: Good: Bad:	**ME**	Name: Good: Bad:	Name: Good: Bad:
Name: Good: Bad:	Name: Good: Bad:	Name: Good: Bad:	Name: Good: Bad:	Name: Good: Bad:
Name: Good: Bad:	Name: Good: Bad:	Name: Good: Bad:	Name: Good: Bad:	Name: Good: Bad:

Draw a line from the ME box to all the things you think you've
inherited from your family – good or bad. You might find
you've got more in common than you think.

READING, LISTENING & WATCHING LIST ON FAMILY

Watching

Television series and films

The Royle Family
Gilmore Girls
Brothers & Sisters
The Goldbergs
The Royal Tenenbaums
Raised by Wolves
Little Miss Sunshine

Reading

The Catcher in the Rye – J. D. Salinger
I Capture the Castle – Dodie Smith
Red Ink – Julie Mayhew
Paper Aeroplanes – Dawn O'Porter
Little Women – Louisa May Alcott

Listening

'We Are Family' – The Pointer Sisters
'Everybody's Free' – Quindon Tarver
'When Doves Cry' – Prince
'Sweet Mother' – Skepta
'It's a Family Affair' – Sly and the Family Stone

16

FRIENDSHIP

I am a map of my friends. A big tangled map of roads, paths, avenues, forests, woods and rivers, each representing the people I love in my life. No one else can make me feel as raucous or as safe, as defiant or as carefree and fun. No one else has the ability to yank me out when I am stuck in a patch of quicksand sadness.

With our friends we are our nuanced* and evolving selves. No matter how large or small your crew of mates is, at any one time

chips are down, who make you laugh and let you cry. A good friend is someone who won't just tell you what you want to hear, but that you can trust not to bullshit you. A good friend knows that you have boundaries and won't cross them.

Imagine you are a bonfire. You need the right wood as your foundation. The bad, rotten, wrong type of wood won't help your flame roar bright. I am in awe of the magic humans I've encountered who keep

YOU'VE GOT A FRIEND

in your life, they are a fragmented mosaic of personality-filled mirrors, reflecting how you want to treat yourself at that time. Different groups of friends make up the chapters to your internal book. They can challenge you if you are being reckless, and they can help you take risks when you need to.

The saying 'choose your friends wisely' is true. Good friends are those who don't pressure or manipulate you, who cheer when you're doing well, and hug you when the

my bonfire alight. My friends make me feel good about who I am most of the time, and it's one of life's biggest pleasures if I can reciprocate that, and help them feel the same.

I hope you are reading this, nodding and feeling the same way too. Think of the people out of all those you call friends that just rock! They sparkle! They are fantastic! Think about the remarkable memories you've made together. Feel proud, as it is a reflection of how fantastic you must be too.

*'Nuance' is one of my favourite words. Here's its definition, in case ya didn't already have its meaning under your belt: **Nuance:** a subtle difference in or shade of meaning, expression or sound.

Who are your friends?
Write their names here:

FANTASTIC FRIENDSHIPS

Word wall, built with a little help from my friends..

MISCHIEF

EASE

LAUGHTER HONESTY

MUTUAL RESPECT

FUN

TRUTH

FORGIVENESS

COMMUNICATION

COMFORTABILITY COMFORT

LOYALTY

A TRUE MATE WILL ALWAYS HAVE YOUR BACK

Once, with one of my best friends – Bri – I gave a talk on the importance of female friendship throughout history. As we started to scratch the surface, we were shocked to find that there aren't many examples that have been documented. There were a couple of examples that I found to be pretty cool, though – as follows:

Anne Bonny and Mary Read

Described as 'fierce hellcats' – Anne Bonny and Mary Read were swashbuckling, filthy, dangerous and rare female pirates in the1700s. Instantly thick as thieves in 1720, when their unbreakable friendship was formed, they set sail the same year on a ship called *Revenge*. Anne was outwardly female, while Mary had had a history of keeping her born gender under wraps, and had joined the military years previously under the name of Mark, dressed as a man. Anne kept Mary's secret for as long as she could (some stories say a romance developed between the pair). That was until Anne's husband, Calico Jack – who was also a pirate on the ship – became too jealous of his wife flirting with 'Mark' onboard.

Anne and Mary's friendship saw them through the rough piracy and crime-filled seas of the West Indies for a year. Together with the rest of the ship's crew they navigated rough seas, fought enemy ships and drank together. In 1721, the ship was finally caught – and all on board were tried for the crime of piracy and were hanged. All, that is, except for Mary and Anne, who both escaped the death sentence by 'pleading the belly' – otherwise known as declaring pregnancy. In jail they had adjoining cells to await the birth of their children. Sadly, Mary died of a ferocious fever before giving birth, while Anne's fate is unknown. BFFs till the bitter end.

B·F·F

Marilyn Monroe and Ella Fitzgerald

A little-known and inspiring tale of female friendship that I stumbled across was that of Hollywood actress Marilyn Monroe and jazz musician Ella Fitzgerald. Back in 1950s America, racism was rife and segregation all too prevalent in many states. Ella, despite being hugely talented and popular, struggled to push through prejudice against the colour of her skin, and was banned from playing many live music venues, purely for being a black woman. A certain notorious club of the time, the Mocambo Nightclub in Los Angeles, was no exception.

Marilyn Monroe, a regular at the club, was so stirred and outraged on learning of Ella's treatment that she rang the owner of the Mocambo personally and demanded they hire Ella immediately, declaring that she, Marilyn, would sit at the front table every night Ella performed. At the time, Marilyn was one of the biggest movie stars on the planet, and she knew her presence would attract the kind of publicity that Mocambo couldn't resist. The club complied, and Marilyn made sure she was there, at the front table every single night that Ella performed. The press went bonkers, and as a result Ella Fitzgerald's success propelled to stratospheric heights. Marilyn and Ella remained good friends.

Friends come in all forms – and the good ones will always have your back, no matter what.

Are you a good friend?

Ask your mates on WhatsApp now what it's like to be your friend! It's daunting, but illuminating. I just did, and I learned that I need to be better at answering my phone to some mates, but that some of my mates find me optimistic – which is nice.

What did you learn from asking your mates what kind of friend you are?

I'M A BIT OF A FLAKY FRIEND

Flake

The late friend

The one you harbour fairly deep annoyance about. You know that they aren't evil, so you can't not be their friend any more. You JUST DON'T understand how they can ALWAYS be THAT late.

The flaky friend

One step further along the toxic scale than the late friend is the FLAKY one. They are just NEVER there when you need them to be. You cannot understand how they always seem to be doing fun things on social media when they always have an excuse to cancel on you at the last minute.

The competitive friend

The one that JUST has to have one up on you. They quash your good news with theirs. They are usually harbouring secret envy – a telltale sign for this being their bruised look every time you tell them about something awesome that has happened to you.

WHO ARE THEY?

The self-obsessed friend

The mate who you know full well you'll be acting as a therapist for whenever you see them. This mate is unlikely to ask you how you are EVER.

The friend you don't trust

. . . with the one you fancy, because they will flirt with them. Also the one who you just know says one thing to one person, another to another, and so on. The friend with MANY faces.

The toxic friend

This is the worst type. The toxic friend makes you feel bad about yourself, puts you down, lets you down, never has your back.

If any of your friends are in the pink zone, then TALK to them about how they make you feel. Chances are they have no idea how their behaviour is affecting you. If any of them are in the red zone, then consider unfriending them. Chances are they know what they are doing and won't change.

BEING BULLIED

Bullying is universal, in schools, places of work, in relationships and online. It makes the bullied feel as small as a shirt button, as alone as a lost plastic bag bobbing around in the wind. It devastates your sense of security. It can make you feel like your world is caving in. It makes you feel powerless.

IT SUCKS.
YOU ARE WORTH MORE.

Bullies are essentially troubled individuals who lack self-esteem and draw their power from making other people feel worthless and small. They are often victims of bullying themselves, so they know how it works. Being bullied feels like you are drowning in irrational hostility and meanness. It can truly overshadow any positivity and joy you feel, and put you in a place where you actually believe that you deserve this treatment.

Don't let the harshness win. It isn't your problem, it's theirs. Remember that bullies are feeling their own pain too. Bullies are people who have not got to the bottom of their darkness. They don't like themselves, but are unable to face up to their problems. Their hearts are hurting too. OUCH. It hurts all round.

But here's the thing: YOU have power, more than you know. You can choose how bullying is dealt with. Switch off your phone, tell someone in authority, call someone out for being a bully. As a type of abuse, bullying is well acknowledged as deeply upsetting and is thankfully now taken very seriously. All bullying is wrong – there is a never a case where it's OK to bully. Things can get better if you try to protect yourself by finding the strength to walk away from this negative behaviour. Never suffer alone: TELL SOMEONE IMMEDIATELY.

If you are a bully, it's time to STOP and work out why you are doing it in the first place. What gives you the right to put someone through this hell? Being kind to people feels so much better.

There is some brilliant anti-bullying information and advice from anti-bullying ambassadors on www.antibullyingpro.com. Head there for more information.

If you'd like some extra help telling someone you are being bullied, please use the letter template below. Either photocopy it, fill in the blanks and post it through the appropriate person's door, or copy it into an email and send it to that person instead.

```
Dear . . .

I've been wanting to tell you that I'm being bullied and it's
starting to really get me down. I wanted to open up. It's been
quite hard to tell anyone because I'm (delete as applicable)
scared/embarrassed/afraid/ashamed/feeling very sad about it.

It is happening as regularly as . . . . . time(s) a week.

It is taking place in the form of (delete as applicable) online
bullying/face-to-face bullying.

Examples
below:.............................................................
...................................................................
...................................................................

I'd like to talk to you more about it.
Please call or email me back on...................................

Thank you. Your support on this would be so hugely appreciated.

From

...................................................................
```

BREAKING UP
WITH FRIENDS

The so-called friends who mostly make you feel ANGUISH and UNCERTAINTY, or have too often LED YOU ASTRAY, are usually better off as friends of the past rather than the present. It's not easy to distance yourself from certain people, but sometimes it's the best thing you can do to protect yourself and your peace of mind. You don't have to be unkind – just don't see them one-on-one any more – make sure it's in wider groups only, so that it's not so intense. Fill your time with activities that you love, and the mates that make you howl with laughter and make you feel good about yourself. You'll soon be 'too busy' to be sucked of energy by a manipulative, stinky bad egg.

BE YOUR OWN
BEST FRIEND

So we've established that your mates are very important. But the fact is that your friendship with YOURSELF is the most important one you'll ever have.

Be your own best friend. Be kind to yourself and take control of how your life plays out. Stop beating yourself up if you make a mistake – learn from mistakes; accept who you are and what makes you tick.

DO THINGS THAT MAKE YOU FEEL GOOD IN YOUR OWN COMPANY:

* Take a dog for a walk
* Have a massage
* Head to the steam room of your local pool
* Try giving yourself a pedicure
* Go and take photos of beautiful things
* Smile at your reflection in the mirror

* Make a gigantic homemade pizza that has so many toppings it looks like a compost bin has exploded
* Knit or crochet a miniature scarf
* Watch a great box set
* Dance alone in your bedroom
* Jump on the bed

* Write – a book, a blog, a diary
* Draw, paint or colour something in
* Read
* Download and listen to an audio book
* Express yourself, however you can and however you want.

Learn self-reliance. It is ace and can help make you strong. It's a way to learn to trust your own instincts and take care of yourself – mind and body. Learning to like your own company and being fully independent is as GOOD for you as finding the love of your life.

Five things I like to do/would like to do by myself.

1)

2)

3)

4)

5)

LOVE

28

Oh cripes. This stuff is the deepest of all.
It's the heavy stuff. But, oh my goodness . . .
When it's GOOD –

it's gooood.

THE REAL THING

So, what about L.O.V.E.? I'm not talking about our obsession with thumping hearts on screens – I'm talking about the real stuff. The dizzying stuff. The stuff that can make you gulp, make your mouth dry up and your face crumple into a squishy, happy sad-clown face. The love that makes you cry and throb. The real love. The romantic type. The most-confusing-of-all type. An emoji just isn't going to work for this.

The love letter to love

Dear Love,

I love you for always being there.

I love how you are only truly described through song and kisses.

Thank you for helping me to patch out some of my flaws and feel totally floored whilst doing it.

I've learned that in your maddest moments it can sometimes be impossible to speak, to think straight, to be afraid of anything, even death.

Thank you for making me understand what it's like to be an insane, raging beast.

Thanks for twisting my morals to help me define them.

Thank you for continuing to return. Even when I think you have gone for good.

Thank you for those moments, when I'm looking for the meaning of life, that I'm reminded it's you.

Love,
Gem

Your love is bespoke, and so is mine. It can mean a different thing to each of us. The reliability and security found in many partnerships is vital for some and not others. It's too easy to fall into a trap of looking around too much – to want to have what others have, purely out of pack mentality. It's important to swim in your own love channel and decide what's right for the rhythm of your own heartbeat.

YOUR LOVE

REAL love can feel like being out of control, and you cannot necessarily always predict WHO you love and HOW you love. Sometimes you want to keep it casual –

sometimes you don't. Sometimes the person you love will want something different from you. No best friend, family member or even book can tell you what to do when it comes to whether YOU should be attracted to someone, get together with someone, break up with someone, get back together with someone, or if you would be better off alone. Your love is your love, and you know it better than anyone. If you're feeling confused by who you love or worried about telling the people around you about them because you think they won't approve, then this is when it's most important to listen to your heart and be guided by it.

. . . No one tells you this, but strong and healthy relationships of all kinds need WORK. Just like plants need care and nurturing to grow. Unfortunately relationships don't come with instructions on how to maintain them – that's something you have to learn all by yourself.

THE WALTZER

Love. Oh yes. It's like being on a waltzer at the funfair:
it's hard to focus, a bit sickening, exciting, thrilling and scary,
and you are definitely not alone if you are . . .

feeling a bit
obsessed with
someone right
now.

desperately
heartbroken and
think you will never be
the same again.

in the wrong
relationship and
need to assess why and
how you might want
to get out.

Keep
reading.

Keep
reading.

Head to page 42
on heartbreak
and what it can and
can't do.

SPLITTING UP IS BORING

Whenever I've split up with someone, it's been because I start to get a headache. My head aches with keeping them happy and with trying to work out why they don't make me feel like myself any more, and it aches even more at the relentless thoughts of splitting up with them.

There is no easy way of splitting up with someone.

EVEN IF YOU CAN'T BE BOTHERED WITH ALL THE MESS THAT COMES WITH BREAKING UP. EVEN THOUGH YOU MIGHT EVEN STILL LOVE THEM. I'M SORRY TO HAVE TO TELL YOU THIS, BUT... IF YOU WANT TO SPLIT UP WITH SOMEBODY, THEN YOU NEED TO DO IT.

Regardless of how much you adore that person's family, or remember the promises you once made to them, or the pet you share, or are worried what your bed will feel like without them in it.

Be brave, rip the plaster off. It will be painful. But, once the rain has stopped, a rainbow may appear.

I'M NOT IN LOVE

Love is fluid, it changes all the time, and if you're lucky it just gets deeper. Some of us need to be 'in love' – we need fireworks and piping hot 'smoochy' times, like in romcoms and songs, or like our friends who seem to 'have it all'. If that doesn't happen straight away, then often we panic and think it can't be right.

Calm down. We have a lifetime to love, and love when it arrives can be beautifully unique, subtle and different from what you've known before. Being 'in love' with a person can happen after a while, when you've really got to know them. When that happens, it's amazing, because it is built on something real, and not just attraction, or brain-mangling infatuation. Attraction is very important, but that might happen later too. Someone can definitely become more attractive the more you know them.

Take your time, and don't rush or make rash decisions. You don't need to verbally commit to anything at all. Chill, sit in the park on a blanket together, get to know each other. You don't need to go running to Vegas to get married. Only do that if it's the real 'holy-moly' deal.

Your life is not a film.

My Story...

MY LOVE

PSSSSSTTTT . . . At the time of writing, I have had five noteworthy partners and fallen in love six different times (two of those times were with the same person). The first time I fell in love I was twelve years old. But love is not about numbers – it's about people. If you were to see each of my loves in a line-up, you would be befuddled by what a hotchpotch you'd see.

I am open to all sorts, as long as I see a magic about them. I've had to learn the hard way about 'Love versus Madness'. Each of my loves impacted on me big. A couple of them impacted on me monstrously. Out of the five, two ended up being toxic for me (typically, I was madly in love with those people at the time). They were dangerous loves that eroded my well-being. (Please head to page 39 for more on abusive relationships.)

The other three are great people with kindness in their hearts who taught me that I am lovable and worthy of someone dreamy and amazing. I will always consider these three loves friends, even if I don't see some of them much any more. And the one I'm with now (who was actually my downstairs neighbour) is a really good one, thank goodness.

If there's one thing I've learned, it's that you never know who you're going to meet, or who you'll fall for in this life, or how it will happen. And that, my friend, is EXCITING.

you turn my legs to jelly.

INFATUATION

Once I was so infatuated with a boy it was painful. I just couldn't wash him out of my hair. I'd think about him all the time. I'd carefully plan what I was going to wear the next time I saw him. Whenever we were near one another, I felt the kind of electric bolts through my body that could create power cuts. I couldn't take my eyes off him in a crowd . . . He drove me crazy. It wasn't exactly fun.

Sometimes this boy chose to talk to me at the end of the night, or to kiss me. Sometimes he didn't. Sometimes he'd choose somebody else to wrap himself around instead. It hurt, but it also made him more intoxicating. He was charismatic, vulnerable and a little mean, but he never failed to make me erupt with laughter.

I talked about this boy a LOT, trying to work out whether he felt the same. In the end a friend of mine got so bored with my infatuation that one day she opened up her computer and played the new song she'd written. It is called 'Dickhead' and is by Kate Nash and you should definitely give it a listen.

The side-effects of
REJECTION

Most of us have been rejected. It is never pleasant. Often, splitting up is not a mutual decision and, if you are the one being 'rejected' or dumped, hopefully it will be done as kindly as possible, so you're not left in a mess. But then there are those who keep you dangling and insecure and never properly commit, only to reject you in the end. If you are chasing after someone who's not totally interested in you, it can seriously rattle your self-esteem. You don't always realize how it is making you feel about yourself at the time, but to be aware of the side-effects of rejection can be helpful and will stop you from beating yourself up about it.

Days or months later, even when you've moved on from that particular person, you may find yourself feeling that you are not attractive or interesting enough, that there's something wrong with you. There is nothing wrong with you, except for the fact that you once tried to love someone who didn't love you back. Your pride took such a hit that it was left dented.

Know this, breathe deep, put your armour back on and head out on your next adventure, keeping your head held high – there are over seven billion people on Planet Earth right now.

You got this.

DISAGREEING WITH THE ONES WE LOVE

Communication and patience are our best tools when it comes to disagreement with those we love.

COMMUNICATION TOOLS

- Put yourself in the other person's shoes and try to understand why they're saying what they are saying.

- Think of ways round expressing your particular opinion without getting angry. Shouting never works.

- Come up with different ways of explaining whatever it is that you are disagreeing about. A letter? A discussion at a later date?

- And, in the meantime, it might be good to get someone else's opinion.

PATIENCE

- Refer to the point opposite on 'discussion at a later date'.

- Time, which comes up a lot in this book, is a magical thing.

- Over time, things can inexplicably fall into place.

- Time really does heal. Patience applied to a disagreement with someone can work wonders.

TOXIC LOVE AND ABUSIVE RELATIONSHIPS

In a 2009 NSPCC survey, one-quarter of girls aged thirteen to seventeen reported experiencing intimate partner violence; one in nine female respondents had experienced severe physical violence; and almost three-quarters of girls had experienced emotional abuse.*

From the age of twelve to seventeen, I was with a boy, the same age as me, who I felt truly, madly, deeply for. We lived every day in the moment, kissed more than anyone's ever kissed, and would've glued ourselves to one another if we could. It was fast, it was ferocious and it was a furious kind of love. It was my first love, which I don't necessarily believe is the best as they say, but I do believe it is the most confusing.

I was young, filled with feelings and learning how to steer it all, how to motor along and function in life as smoothly as I could. Sometimes it was really, really good – and sometimes it was really, really bad. Sometimes we'd argue so much he'd get really angry; he'd smack my head against the wall in his bedroom. Or he'd squeeze my thigh so hard under the table to secretly threaten me that it would bruise.

What I couldn't identify at the time was that I was in a DAMAGING and ABUSIVE relationship. I felt so wrapped up in my own world and in our own moment that when these bad things happened, all I wanted most in the world was for him to say sorry (which he never did). I didn't think about how it would make me feel years later, after we'd broken up. I had no idea that what was going on with us was proper abuse – at the time, the only abuse I saw represented anywhere was related to older people, married couples, mostly on soaps like *Brookside*. I never saw anything I identified with – nothing that showed my situation.

I was fifteen. I had no idea of the seriousness. I wish someone could've told me how bad it was, that I was letting him do this to me over and over. I wish someone could've told me that it wasn't my fault and that I didn't deserve it. It took me finding him in bed with not one, but two other girls to finally break up with him, I'm ashamed to say – it wasn't even the violence. It was only years later that I realized how toxic he was for me.

I would NEVER let ANYONE use their physical strength against me ever, ever again.

I now passionately believe in highlighting the issue of violent and abusive relationships amongst teenagers and young people.

*Abuse: to use (something) to bad effect or for a bad purpose; misuse.

A few years ago I was in a shop in East London – where I was living at the time – and I overheard a conversation between two schoolgirls about pop stars Rihanna and Chris Brown. It had recently been globally reported that Chris Brown (nineteen at the time) had attacked his then girlfriend Rihanna (twenty-one at the time) and left her face badly beaten.

'Did you hear about what happened to Rihanna?' said one of the girls.

'No. What happened?' asked her friend.

'Chris Brown beat the crap out of her,' the other responded nonchalantly.

'Bet she deserved it, the slag,' said her friend.

Hearing this conversation nearly made me burst into tears – it brought back how I had never taken my own abusive relationship seriously either. It made me want to investigate the attitudes of young people when it comes to what's OK, and what is not OK.

So I made a documentary about it for Radio 1. It was called 'Bruising Silence', and it focused on the nuances of abusive relationships, our understanding of them, and what defines abusive from a young person's perspective.

Making the documentary was as fascinating as it was sad. I interviewed many different people on the subject of abusive relationships. I learned that unfortunately there are many different foul flavours of abuse.

Abuse does not discriminate and can happen in all types of relationships, including same-sex relationships.

- A female can be the abuser as well as a male.

- It can be nearly impossible to detect subtle abuse, the type that is more mental rather than physical or verbal.

- Abuse has many layers and can make someone feel powerless.

- Abuse can even exist in loving relationships.

All abuse is very serious. I want you to know that if someone is hurting you, mentally or physically, it is not right and that you must seek extra help.

WHAT DOES COERCIVE MEAN?

'Coercive' is a word describing a form of control of a dysfunctional nature. It is associated with threats, and bullying. Someone in a coercive relationship may not be able to recognize the signs easily and it can be done in a swirl of seemingly gentle ways. Like when someone makes you feel like you 'HAVE TO . . .' do something, go somewhere, be a certain way. If you are ever feeling you 'HAVE TO . . .' any of these things ask yourself who's applying the pressure and how often that happens.

It is not easy to understand the curves and the bends of relationships, but 'stock checks' are important. Assessing if you're genuinely happy most of the time needs to happen lots, even in the most loving of relationships.

Women's Aid says:

If you think you might be in an abusive relationship, remember you are not on your own and it is not your fault. You can go to www.lovedontfeelbad.co.uk to find out more about different forms of abuse, including coercive and controlling behaviour, and how you can get support and information. You can also go to the main Women's Aid website – www.womensaid.org.uk – to visit our Survivors' Forum, where you can speak to others who have experienced abuse in a relationship, or call the National Domestic Violence Helpline on 0808 2000 247, which runs in partnership with Women's Aid and Refuge.

HEARTBREAK

ACHY BREAKY HEART

Most of the human race has experienced heartache. MILLIONS of people have had their hearts broken. It's a completely normal part of life, and an important part too. Artists, poets and musicians have done their best work during or after heartbreak (more on this later). Heartbreak means you are ALIVE. You feel things. And you will grow through it all. It makes you the amazing person you are, one who has empathy and compassion.

THE RULES OF HEARTBREAK AND HEARTACHE

**A HEART can ACHE
for a number of reasons.**

Injustice in the world

A natural disaster

A smell

A movie

A song

A letter

Loss

**And A HEART can BREAK because of
a number of triggers.**

A person or an animal you love dying

A person betraying you

A friend dropping you

Global tragedies such as wars, terrorism,
   droughts, poverty or accidents

Anyone you care for being seriously ill

Being dumped

And HOW does it FEEL?

Like your world has caved in

Like a part of you is missing

Like the sun has gone in forever

Like happiness will never come back

Like a pain in your chest, or your stomach

Like your tears will never stop

It HURTS SO BAD.
**But it WILL get better. And it
will not kill you – it will make
you stronger.**

HEARTBREAK CAN...

- **turn you into a bit of beast,** a crying, snotty, wailing heartbreak monster – a stomping, angry, wild thing.

- **make you react extremely emotionally** to songs that wouldn't usually affect you.

- **do the same as above, but with sad or romantic films,** especially on planes for some reason. You can find yourself on a flight with an uncontrollably tear-drenched face (this has happened to me SO many times).

- **dent your pride.** You'll find that your ego is at a loose end when breaking up, even though sometimes a relationship just simply ISN'T RIGHT.

- **make you lose your appetite.** But please do eat – it'll make you feel better. Eat some ice cream.

- **confuse the hell out of you.** It's even possible to fancy someone harder when they are unattainable – a cruel and twisted element of fate.

- **make you engage in some hard snogging with your ex,** even though you are likely to crash and burn afterwards.

- **chemically imbalance you.** Some research has shown that breaking up with someone can be similar to the feeling of withdrawing from actual drugs. GAHHHH.

- **hurt.** It's been proven that heartbreak can create a physical pain and discomfort, like a tight chest, stomach pain or headache.

- **make you go off the things you used to love,** like sunshine, or chips.

- **radically change your appearance,** or cause you to take up exercise obsessively, anything to distract yourself!

- **give you the most refreshing newfound sense of independence.**

- **make you wiser and stronger.**

HEARTBREAK CAN'T...

- stay forever.

- stop you from fancying someone else.

- **stop you from being clever and funny and creative,** or good at maths. You are bright like a spark – if not brighter now.

- **be shaken off easily.** Give yourself the time you need to heal. Time will make it easier, and sometimes a good actual shake is worth a try.

- **be fully described in emoji form.** If you are ready to use these to describe how you feel, I reckon you're feeling a bit better.

- **always be completely understood by everyone around you.** Sometimes our mates and family members just won't understand how we feel. Don't expect everyone to always get it.

- **stop you from being beautiful.** You are still beautiful.

- **stop the world from spinning on its axis.** Even though it feels like the world doesn't look the same during heartbreak, it is still there, waiting for you.

- **sink your boat.** It's been rocked, but it can't sink it.

46 ♥

Pharmacy Stamp	Age	Title, Forename, Surname & Address
	D.O.B.	

Number of days' treatment
N.B. Ensure dose is stated

Endorsements

SYMPTOMS: Loud crying, hyper sensitivity, feeling sorry for yourself and wrapping yourself up into a hedgehog-like ball.

DIRECTIONS: Invite every single one of your friends to your house immediately, moan about your heartbreak till you have no words left. Then cover your face in glitter and go out disco-dancing in the sparkliest outfit you own, and dance till it feels like your legs might drop off.

REPEAT EVERY WEEKEND TILL YOU ARE FEELING BETTER.

Signature of Prescriber

Date

For dispenser No. of Prescns. on form

Gemma Cairney

YOUR HEARTACHE PLAYLIST

**Melt into the magic of music
with a specially prepared
HEARTBREAK PLAYLIST.**

For a good cry

1. 'Thinkin' 'Bout You' –
    Frank Ocean
2. 'Never Ever' – All Saints
3. 'Don't Speak' – No Doubt
4. 'Radio Silence' –
    James Blake
5. 'No Room for Doubt'
    by Lianne La Havas and
    Willy Mason
6. 'Mood Indigo' –
    Nina Simone

For hopes and boogies

1. 'Daydreamer' – Adele
2. 'Tears Dry On Their Own' –
    Amy Winehouse
3. 'Shake It Out' – Florence
    and The Machine
4. 'Shackles' – Mary Mary
5. 'Heartbreaker' –
    Mariah Carey
6. 'Shine On' – Roses
7. 'Dancing On My Own' –
    Robyn

Help for heartache

Most heartache will pass, but if you are finding it VERY difficult to move forward and feel stuck with your feelings, or if you are worried about your mental health, head to the 'YOUR MIND' section of this book.

Always ask for help.

DEATH, LOSS AND GRIEF

A RICH AND CONFUSING PAIN

We can learn a lot about how we feel about life from death. Death can make you angrier and more confused and helpless than anything else. Death leaves us desperate. It is the one inevitable truth about life. It is the darkest of dark, the biggest blow – the deepest.

The fear of death is in most of us. It's hard to admit – if we admit it, it may envelop our entire being and we won't be able to shake the thought. Fear of being alone, fear of loss, fear of fear.

WHEN SOMEBODY DIES

Grief is as individual as we are. There is no right way to do it. No right or wrong feeling. When somebody you love dies, the first thing you feel is shock, even if you know it is coming. You might feel nothing at first, and that is OK. Let yourself work through it at your own pace. If you want to cry, feel free to stoop your head, and give yourself to the sadness.

I will never forget the puddles of tears and sticky wet faces during the periods of bereavement in my life. It hurts like a dagger to lose someone. It hurts to watch others hurting who've lost someone too. I've always found a warmth in togetherness during these times. To know that neither I nor whoever it is that's lost someone close to them is alone.

I don't think the hurt ever completely goes away. But time makes it less raw. I promise you. Never, ever forget that there is someone out there that wants to soothe your ache. There are people who will open their ears to you no matter how bleak you feel.

No right or wrong feeling

TRYING TOO HARD TO GET OVER IT

Feeling like you have to be fine straight away, bounce back and get on with work and normal life can affect you later down the line. Ride the waves of your heart, check in with yourself daily. You might feel completely different day by day or hour by hour, and people around you will just have to go with it. If you feel like you need some time to yourself, you need it.

On the other hand, wanting to be happy again is not wrong either. It is also completely normal. You have a life to live, and if something makes you giggle that is all right, that's what the person you've lost would've wanted – for you to still know what it's like to giggle. Don't ever feel guilty about how you feel – guilt is a waste of time.

WHAT TO EXPECT

I talked to a young woman called Frances Acquaah, who is the primary carer for her younger brother and sister since the death of her dad six years ago, and her mother more recently. Frances opened up to me about her experiences.

'Time is a healer,' says Frances. 'Many people will tell you. I found this especially annoying because I couldn't see past how I felt in that very moment. Take it each day at a time. Do not let anyone rush you or tell you how you should feel. Whilst I don't believe there is a "one size fits all" guide of what to expect, here are a few things I experienced after losing my parents.'

CHANGE

'When you lose someone, especially someone that you love or are close to, everything changes. In my personal experience, there is no way you can be prepared for this, even if this person's death was expected.

'When my mother passed away, everything changed. Most of it was stuff that was out of my control, and it was challenging to adjust to my new life and responsibilities. It's so easy to bury your head under the sand – as I did initially – but the longer you do this, the harder it will be when you have to face your new realities.

'Whilst it's important to take time out and address your feelings, it's equally important to have someone around to keep your affairs in order until you're ready.'

ANXIETY

'I avoided social situations for a long time. I didn't want people to tell me they were "sorry" and I hated the way people treated me with pity. Apart from this, my emotions were unpredictable. I could feel completely numb one day, and spend the next week crying myself to sleep. I'm the type of person that likes to block things out (I wouldn't advise anyone to do this, by the way), but I've been learning to accept how I feel in every moment, even if that means crying in public! Remember you are a human being and not a robot.'

DENIAL

'Dealing with grief when you are young, it can be hard to accept that they are gone. Denial is often spoken about as a key stage of the grieving process, and it is definitely something I've encountered more so the second time around.

'I was seventeen when my father died. He wasn't very well, so it was a lot easier to accept his death over my mother's, whom I was closer to. Sometimes I just sit in disbelief, as I still can't believe she isn't here. I once even thought about ringing her to tell her something – then I remembered I couldn't.

'Even now, just over a year later, I tend to speak about my mum in the present tense. Is this healthy? I'm no expert, but this is how I feel comfortable talking about her for now, so that's what I'm going to do.'

DEPRESSION

'I'm not sure what words can be used to accurately describe the feeling of losing someone you love. It's a heart-wrenching feeling that makes the world stop for you.

'I think it's important to seek help when you're feeling low, regardless of how you got to that place. But you have to be ready and open to receive help. Admitting it is the hardest part. Once you've done this, you are well on your way!

'Getting the help you need can often be a bit tricky, but don't be disheartened if your doctor fails you or if you are turned away – keep trying! Whilst counselling didn't solve my problems, I did, however, find it helpful to talk about how I was feeling and say the words out loud.'

BEING THERE FOR YOUR GRIEVING FRIENDS

It's not easy to know how to support people you love when they are grieving. Here's some useful advice of what to do, and what not to do.

Be positive

Don't project your fear of death on to them. Nobody who's recently lost someone wants to hear how much you'd hate it if it happened to you. Nor do they necessarily expect you to know exactly how it feels. The truth is you don't know exactly, because we're all different.

Hug and comfort

Hug them tight and ask them if they are all right. Refer to the reading list for loss and grieving on page 56, and perhaps choose one book to give them as a gift?

Listen

There is no right or wrong in the subject of dying – just keep close and listen to how they feel, and be prepared to feel stilted at points. No one has the answers, but those who are grieving don't want to feel ostracized for doing so.

INGREDIENTS FOR A HAPPY HEART

All you need for a happy heart is to approach life's situations with an OPEN heart. A heart full of empathy, kindness, compassion and hope.

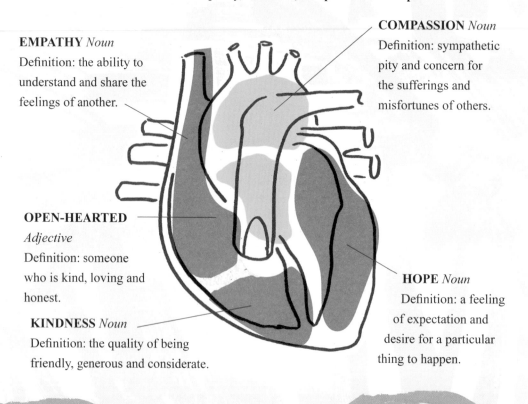

EMPATHY *Noun*
Definition: the ability to understand and share the feelings of another.

COMPASSION *Noun*
Definition: sympathetic pity and concern for the sufferings and misfortunes of others.

OPEN-HEARTED
Adjective
Definition: someone who is kind, loving and honest.

KINDNESS *Noun*
Definition: the quality of being friendly, generous and considerate.

HOPE *Noun*
Definition: a feeling of expectation and desire for a particular thing to happen.

READING LIST FOR LOSS AND GRIEVING

My Sister Lives on the Mantlepiece by Annabel Pitcher
Unboxed by Non Pratt
The Square Root of Summer by Harriet Reuter Hapgood
I'll Give You the Sun by Jandy Nelson
The Sky Is Everywhere by Jandy Nelson
The Five Stages of Andrew Brawley by Shaun David Hutchinson
The Year of the Rat by Clare Furniss
A Monster Calls by Patrick Ness

For any more information on bereavement and grief, turn to the back of this book, and you will find organizations there to help you through it.

YOUR MIND

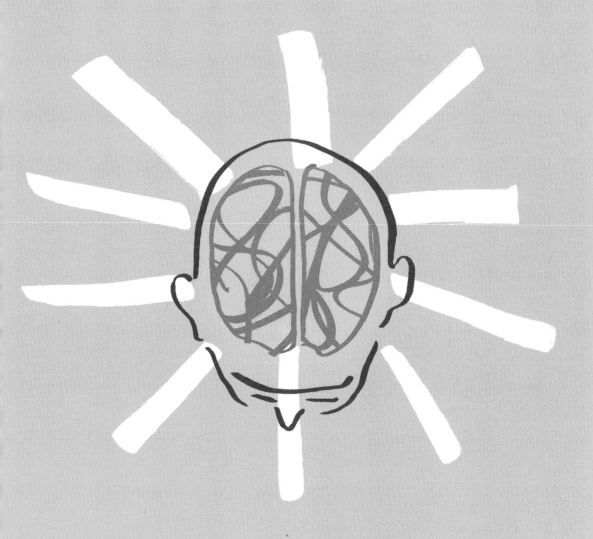

Your mind is your dazzling, powerful control centre – like NASA navigating the vastness of space, or the control tower at every airport coordinating a bajillion planes. The brilliant, boggling headquarters that is your **brain** enables your body to function. KAPOW! WOW! . . . Your brain is immense! It sends thousands of very important signals, every split second, to all parts of your body. Your brain is the most intricate, clever, complex and AMAZING organ you have. Your mind is what makes you an individual. It's what makes you you.

HOUSE

While you're growing – from birth to adult-hood – your brain is developing impressively fast. You learn to crawl, to speak, to read and write, to ride a bike . . . to drive, to cook, to perhaps even speak another language. Your brain is exotic, inquisitive and capable of all sorts. You are endlessly grabbing at the multiple learning opportunities the world around you has to offer with the help of your brain. Stop and give your incredible mind some credit for a second.

You may feel like a loser sometimes – but you were once merely a tiny cell . . . and now look at you! Snap, crackle, POP! – your brain is whirring. If you're lucky, and you protect it, your brain will serve you well. Combined with positive experiences, education, nurturing and the right people around you, your brain will help you make important life decisions, alert you to danger and keep you on the right path.

But sometimes, through no fault of your own, your brain can let you down.

This section of the book will walk you through some important truths about the way our minds work. We'll explore some of the darker corners, and give you the knowledge and the tools to cope when things go wrong. Please read on, especially if you are experiencing issues with your mental health or feeling at a loss in trying to help out a family member or friend.

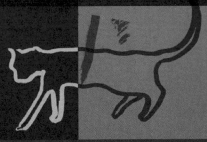

RANDOM
BRAIN-FACT KLAXON . . .
THE REASON YOU CAN'T TICKLE
YOURSELF IS BECAUSE YOUR BRAIN
CAN INSTANTLY DISTINGUISH BETWEEN
UNEXPECTED EXTERNAL TOUCH AND YOUR OWN.
YOUR BRAIN IS WELL CLEVER!

FYI— I love
tickling people.

If we think about ourselves as
brains . . . the brain is a lot
about thinking, but the brain
is also a lot about feeling.
In fact, in Western society we
have an obsession sometimes with
the brain as a thinking thing,
you know, in terms of exams, in
terms of being smart, in terms
of wordiness and so on — and so
on — but actually there's as much
of the brain dedicated to feeling
as there is to thinking.

Dan Glaser, neuroscientist

Understanding your brain and your mind ain't
half TOUGH sometimes.

62

DO YOU EVER FEEL LIKE YOUR HEAD IS IN A CLAMP?

Do you sometimes feel so overwhelmed by life that your mind feels numb and dumb? Are you weary from just thinking so much? Do you feel rinsed out from asking yourself so many questions?

Am I doing the right thing? Do I have the right feeling? What do I eat? Who do I love? Am I working hard enough at my studies, my job, at being a good friend or partner or family member?

I grant you this moment to scream. Yes, SCREAM. OK, don't alarm your neighbours into thinking you are being attacked. But just let it out, that vital and necessary SCREAM . . . Do it into a pillow, or on a rollercoaster, during an orgasm, playing sport or underwater at your local swimming pool. If you feel like life is getting truly annoying, it's OK to scream responsibly.

LIFE ISN'T ALWAYS easy

'Well, it's weird, isn't it?' said my friend Laurence recently, whilst sat around a dinner table philosophizing and trying to work out the meaning of life. 'Being heaps of bones encased in flesh and filled with feelings.'

We were pondering political doom and whether we were making the right life choices. Let's face it: being human is weird. It's weird to sometimes panic that life is too short – and then at other times wish time away. It's weird to want everything to be perfect, but not know what perfect is. We are big, walking, talking contradictions really. Let's just accept that and try to find a middle ground, some calm and acceptance . . .

It is NOT good for your mind to . . .

- bitch about others

- obsessively check in with your phone, rather than your real life

- worry about something out of your physical control

- judge others

- do things that you fundamentally don't agree with – just to please others.

DEMONS

65

Demons. Those nagging obstacles to your peace of mind. They are snarling, weaselly, toad-like things, and they are annoying to say the least. They wield defiant little pickaxes, and their mission is to get right into your noggin,* making you anxious, stressed and upset.

*__Noggin__: a word my cherub of a friend Georgia uses to describe our heads. I love it because it makes our heads seem almost funny.

These demons don't half piss me off, and when I imagine what mine might look like I imagine jumping, blobby, chewed-up bubble-gum balls with poppy-out eyes and big, licking tongues. We each have our own particular demon(s), made up of many things. If we were labelling their ingredients – what they're made up of – they'd contain half a tablespoon of nature (things we are born with – our DNA and genetic make-up), a dash of nurture (how we are brought up, environmental influences), a sprinkling of regret, perhaps the odd trauma and a dollop of fear thrown in for good measure.

Depending on how big and defiant they are, demons are pretty good at getting in the way of life, and they can make us feel out of control. Some people's demons manifest as a sense of isolation; others come as startling anxiety or a panic attack. Some appear as a dark cloud of depression, or as an addiction that grips. Demons are bespoke.

It's good to equip ourselves by KNOWING OUR DEMONS and how they make us feel. Stare them in the face and figure out exactly what we're scared of . . . and – most importantly – WHY we're scared of whatever it might be.

To put it simply: if we can identify the roots of our problems, they aren't as likely to bubble up to boiling point inside us.

Opening up about your demons – big and small – is the first step to getting on better with those pesky toads. There is nothing to be ashamed of: you are a human being, you are dealing with a lot and it's time to offload.

What do your demons look like? Draw them below.

FYI . . .

. . . SINCE CAVE TIMES, we have been tuned in to risk and danger. 'Fight or flight', as the survival response is known, was once upon a time about hunting for food and not getting eaten – these days, our anxiety is about exams, money and terrorism. Some of us soak it up more than others. For some, **fear and anxiety** are all too familiar, and **calmness and happiness** seem harder to find. If this is you – THIS DOESN'T MEAN your life is crap. If this applies to someone you know – and that someone finds reaching a calm mental state a struggle – it doesn't make them less of a person . . . it's just the way their brain is wired.

THE BIG DEMON DETONATORS

The main factors that feed your demons and that can mess with your mental health are:

STRESS
TRAUMA
ANXIETY

They can be caused by external factors such as:

- **Other human beings inflicting pain on to or adding pressure to our lives.**
- **Media/advertising.**
- **Pressure and expectation to achieve/look/behave a certain way.**
- **Traumatic experiences.**

These factors are sometimes out of our control. When we are feeling unhappy, it can be difficult to define why, or to put a finger on exactly where our unhappiness is coming from. These things can swirl together, turning our heads into a pot of steaming mashed potato. Sometimes it is really hard to know what's going on.

I am no stranger to the mashed potato swirl myself. I wear my heart right out and fleshy on my sleeve. I think deeply. I cry deeply. I feel truly, madly, deeply on occasion. Sometimes, this dramatic streak in my nature has threatened to overwhelm me. The plus side of having a mind like mine is it means I have an extraordinary imagination – sometimes my head feels like it contains fireworks.

These days, as a grown woman, I mostly feel genuinely humbled by the brilliance of life and the beautiful things about it – like friendships, conversations and the limitlessness of creativity – all of which keep me warm, happy and feeling safe. But that is now. My lowest point was some time ago – in my early twenties, during a period of big confusion, growing pains, abusive relationships and raw grief. Like many others, I was prescribed antidepressants. Personally, medication wasn't for me. I knew that I needed to deal with my muddled mass of feelings another way.

Led by instinct, I spent time scouring 'alternative therapy' options online and came across a course of 'tapping therapy', which I personally found amazing.

Alternative therapies don't have to cost a lot of money. At that time, I was broke, so I searched HIGH AND LOW to find someone who would help for no more per treatment than it would cost me to go to the cinema. Before you embark on ANY type of therapy, you do need to make sure that you are going to someone both recommended and qualified. So do your research, especially before you embark on alternative therapies. They're not for everyone, but in my opinion – when it comes to matters of the mind – they can be worth investigating and fun to explore.

'I have never met anyone who wanted to feel better so much,' said the angelic alternative therapy lady, who yanked me out of my hole of misery. And all by tapping me whilst I cried. It worked for me.

Please note: Medication is vital for many who suffer from depression and other mental-health-related conditions. It helps them function, and it can save lives. If you have been prescribed antidepressants, please talk to your doctor if you feel you don't need them, and certainly before you stop taking them.

To make better sense of the demon detonators, it helps to know exactly what they are and how they present themselves.

Note: Dr Caroline Taylor, a chartered clinical psychologist, has provided the science bits!

WHAT IS STRESS?

THE SCIENCE BIT:

70

Stress is the experience of being overwhelmed with what we need to do, or think we need to do. Stress happens when we think we don't have the skills, or time, to achieve these things. Unfortunately, thinking that we are unable to do something, and worrying or feeling scared about our perceived inability, makes us more stressed, and so more overwhelmed.

My non-scientific explanation:

Stress is a bit like being in a pressure cooker (I imagine, anyway – as, strangely, I've never been in a pressure cooker!). Your palms might sweat, or you might wake up in a worry fog that you can't shift. When I'm stressed, I can feel adrenalized, a bit helpless, sometimes downbeat, and then guilty about feeling those things – sometimes all at the same time.

WHAT IS ANXIETY?

THE SCIENCE BIT:

Anxiety is the bodily and emotional response to danger or threat. It gives us important information about the situation we are currently in. Anxiety arrives when a hormone called adrenaline is released into our bodies in the face of danger. It often feels very uncomfortable, and makes us want to get away from the emotion and the danger. In this sense, anxiety is our friend — it keeps us safe. If we 'suffer' from anxiety, it is likely that we believe that something will harm us or is a danger to us. Our brain is fine-tuned to stay alert for danger at any given moment, to keep us alive and well. But this means our brain is always searching for threats — and when it finds one it releases adrenaline, even if there is no real danger to our lives. For example, we might get anxious when we revise — not because learning is life-threatening, but because we fear not passing the exam, and the impact that would have on our future.

My non-scientific explanation:

Hurricane-like swirls of anxiety inside us make it feel really difficult to get on with things that we might otherwise find 'easy' – like interacting with people, working or getting from one place to another. These feelings can be described as panic attacks, and they can feel frightening . . . but they do pass.

THE SCIENCE BIT:

Trauma means harm or damage, whether it be physical, psychological, emotional — or all three at the same time. So, for example, someone could be physically injured in a road traffic accident, and be psychologically damaged by the experience — especially if they thought they (or someone they were with) were going to die (or did die). Physical trauma is generally easier to treat than emotional or psychological trauma, mainly because the effects of the physical trauma are easier to understand and see.

72

My non-scientific explanation:

Like a savings bank made up of fear and sadness in your head, trauma can result in phobia, discomfort and pain stored up in our brains. It can be triggered by even the tiniest thing, by our brain's association with whatever ingredients are at the root of our trauma. It is important to identify what these ingredients and triggers are and to recognize what is happening to you. Only then can you give yourself the care you need.

PLEASE REMEMBER: If you can identify with any of this stuff, you are definitely not mad or bad. No one is completely OK all the time. Life affects us in different ways, and our mental health is easily challenged. If and when it is challenged severely, it can be deeply painful and confusing and, most importantly, it can affect your behaviour, your perspective and your ability to cope.

No one's mind reacts to the world in exactly the same way, but if you've experienced any of these demon detonators then you might find that the balance between bleakness and brightness in your brain feels a bit wonky. If that is the case for you or someone you know, then read on. The next section covers the different ways your brain can react to your demons.

SOCIAL ANXIETY DISORDER

It's OK to be you, however you are. It's OK to be shy. But social anxiety is more than shyness. If you are consistently feeling shy or awkward or anxious to an overwhelming degree and it is preventing you from identifying the joy to be found in life, then you may be suffering from something more serious than everyday anxiety.

I hear it from many different types of people. About how the world goes echoey, how it feels like it might burst, how you try to speak but the words won't come out right, because you are unexpectedly afraid of all that is around you. That body-tightening moment of despair at just how crippling social anxiety can be. But when does it become a disorder?

73

Signs of social anxiety disorder

Anxiety from time to time – like when you meet someone new, or you fancy someone, or you have been looking forward to an event for zonks, forever and ever, and then it arrives and you are a ball of anxiety – is part of life. But if it's reaching a stage where it stops you from having fun it's time to work on it.

What to look out for . . .

If you find that you are often tearful – which is seemingly unconnected to any significant or tangible event – or have consistent difficulty in controlling your emotions, or fear going to school or college or taking part in related activities, then these could be signs of social anxiety disorder.

It is important that you can talk to someone openly and honestly about how you feel.

One thing that's good to know is that it's pretty common. Social anxiety disorder is estimated to affect between **ten to fifteen per cent** of people in their lifetime.* Like most of the curves and bends of our minds, the root cause of social anxiety disorder is not always easy to pinpoint in individuals. It could be linked to any 'shake up' of one's life, like a particular event, but it also may not appear to have any link – it is just a gradual accumulation of anxiety.

*Stats from Anxiety Care UK

Do you find yourself excessively worrying about:

How you come across?

What people think of you?

The first impression you give?

Upsetting people?

Something you previously said or did?

74

These worries can build, or spiral to:

- a dread of meeting strangers
- anxiety about or great difficulty in talking to or starting a conversation amongst friends or peers
- anxiety about talking to people in authority, such as teachers or family members
- anxiety about or difficulty with romantic relationships
- studying at school or college, or work
- lack of self-esteem
- drug or alcohol misuse specifically to reduce anxiety

If you're nodding at some of these, then it's time to deal with it. If you haven't told anyone you feel like this, it's time to let those who care about you help and guide you through this time in your life. The strongest mental grip can become looser once you've told people the truth about how hard you find things. Also, talk to yourself. I know this sounds weird, but naming your feelings to yourself out loud really shrinks the power they have over you. Write them down too if you want – to keep in touch with how you feel.

A place to write down your feelings

75

If someone you know has social anxiety disorder, remember:

In extreme cases social anxiety disorder can have a disruptive or disabling impact on a person's life. It can severely affect their confidence and self-esteem, interfere with their relationships and impair their performance at work or school. Be patient and tell the person you know they find certain things hard and that that's OK.

Panic attacks and social anxiety disorder

The fear of a social situation or just thinking about things that you are anxious about can sometimes build up to a panic attack, where you experience an overwhelming sense of anxiety and dread. Panic attacks affect different people in different ways, but often cause physical symptoms such as feeling sick, sweating, trembling and heart palpitations. RUBBISH, right? RIGHT, but though alarming, KNOW THIS . . .

- Panic attacks are **NOT** life-threatening.
- The symptoms often **pass quickly**.
- **Help** is all around you – lots of people know how rubbish panic attacks can be and will be happy to help. Whether that's **putting a hand on your shoulder** or leaving you alone for some time to **breathe** or getting you some **water** and being **by your side** . . . Whatever is best for you.
- The most important thing is that you express how you feel and tell people around you what you need from them.

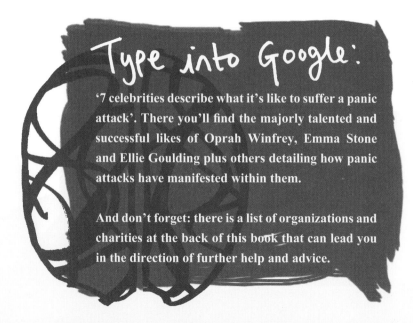

Type into Google:

'7 celebrities describe what it's like to suffer a panic attack'. There you'll find the majorly talented and successful likes of Oprah Winfrey, Emma Stone and Ellie Goulding plus others detailing how panic attacks have manifested within them.

And don't forget: there is a list of organizations and charities at the back of this book that can lead you in the direction of further help and advice.

DEPRESSION

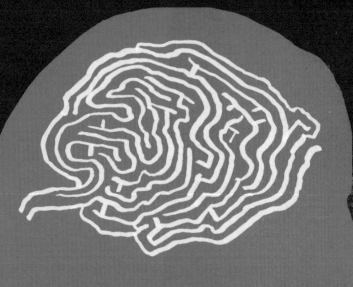

When I was at my lowest ebb, I worried that I was a burden to my friends and family. I feared that if I voiced the pain that I was feeling that they would grow tired of me, or that I would, in turn, bring them down too. Of course I was wrong — people want to help, they want to be there, and if you give them the chance they might just surprise you. At the time, I didn't believe this possible. I shrank into myself, and by doing so I gave the power over to my anxiety and OCD, isolating myself further and retreating under the duvet in an attempt to drown out my spiralling thoughts with only Kirsty Young and Desert Island Discs for company. Every morning I would wake, exhausted, after only a couple of hours' sleep, and wish with my whole heart that somebody was there to hold my hand and say, 'Me too.' That was the catalyst for starting #itaffectsme, to let anyone who is suffering with ill mental health know that they are not alone, that there is an army of us fighting, and that, with talking and help, they can get through it, ten seconds at a time. **"**

Laura Darrall: mental health activist/writer/ actor/kicker of stigma's butt. Founder of the #itaffectsme viral mental health campaign

Mental illness has no prejudices about who it affects, so we should have no prejudices about it.

I asked SANE UK – an awesome, proactive leading mental health charity – to help me break down and define DEPRESSION.

WHAT IS DEPRESSION?

Depression is different from feeling low and unhappy. It can be triggered by difficult life events, such as bereavement, loss of job or financial worries. But it can also occur when there is no obvious reason due to a chemical imbalance in your brain.

It can vary from person to person, but typically if someone is experiencing low mood, and difficulty sleeping or eating over a period longer than two weeks, then they should consider seeing their GP.

HOW CAN WE IDENTIFY IT?

It is important to remember that unless you are a mental-health specialist, you are not qualified to make a diagnosis.

But if you do have concerns for someone who is showing these kinds of symptoms it is a good idea to try to gently encourage them to seek professional help through their GP or other qualified specialist.

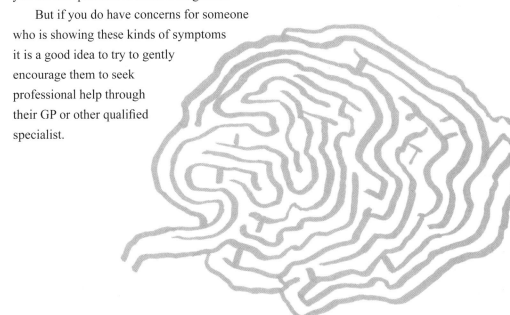

What does SANE UK do
to help those who are depressed?

SANE provides emotional support and information to anyone affected by mental-health problems like depression, including families, friends and carers.

SANEline is a telephone helpline, which is open every evening, every day of the year. There is also a Textcare service that provides supportive text messages at times of need, and an online Support Forum where people can share their experiences and give and receive moral support.

For more information about the services **SANE UK** provides, please visit **www.sane.org.uk**

EATING DISORDERS

FOOD. How do you feel about it?

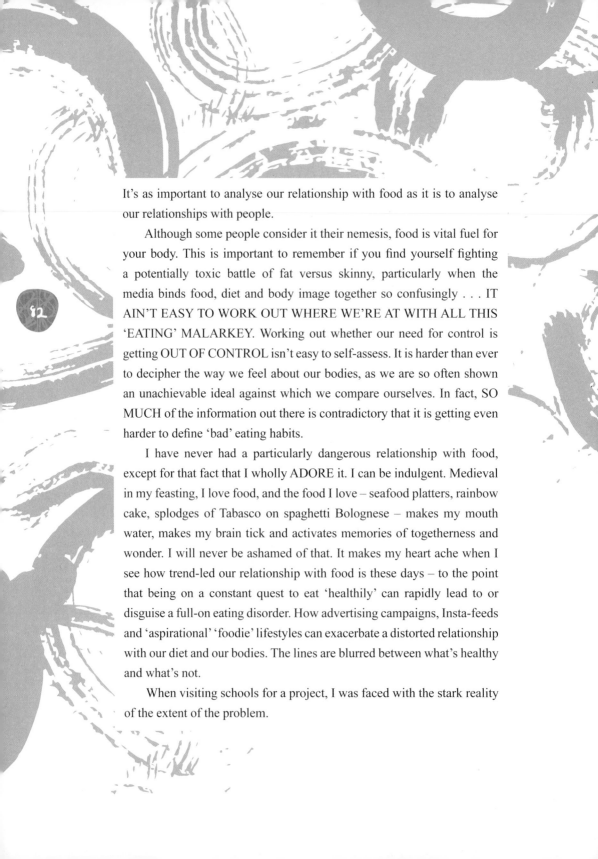

It's as important to analyse our relationship with food as it is to analyse our relationships with people.

Although some people consider it their nemesis, food is vital fuel for your body. This is important to remember if you find yourself fighting a potentially toxic battle of fat versus skinny, particularly when the media binds food, diet and body image together so confusingly . . . IT AIN'T EASY TO WORK OUT WHERE WE'RE AT WITH ALL THIS 'EATING' MALARKEY. Working out whether our need for control is getting OUT OF CONTROL isn't easy to self-assess. It is harder than ever to decipher the way we feel about our bodies, as we are so often shown an unachievable ideal against which we compare ourselves. In fact, SO MUCH of the information out there is contradictory that it is getting even harder to define 'bad' eating habits.

I have never had a particularly dangerous relationship with food, except for that fact that I wholly ADORE it. I can be indulgent. Medieval in my feasting, I love food, and the food I love – seafood platters, rainbow cake, splodges of Tabasco on spaghetti Bolognese – makes my mouth water, makes my brain tick and activates memories of togetherness and wonder. I will never be ashamed of that. It makes my heart ache when I see how trend-led our relationship with food is these days – to the point that being on a constant quest to eat 'healthily' can rapidly lead to or disguise a full-on eating disorder. How advertising campaigns, Insta-feeds and 'aspirational' 'foodie' lifestyles can exacerbate a distorted relationship with our diet and our bodies. The lines are blurred between what's healthy and what's not.

When visiting schools for a project, I was faced with the stark reality of the extent of the problem.

'I only have a miso soup every day for lunch,' said one sixteen-year-old girl, as though she thought it was completely normal.

'But why only that?' I asked.

'Because, I don't want to be fat,' she replied — again in the most chilling, matter-of-fact manner.

It felt like it was only once she voiced this truth that she realized how extreme it sounded. In effect she was starving herself, but most of her peers accepted it as completely normal for her to be monitoring her eating in such a way – the fear of getting fat was far greater than the fear of malnutrition, and a far more relatable idea. I was alarmed. On further investigation, I discovered that she and a friend could sit on Tumblr for up to six hours at a time typing in the word 'skinny' – hours of brainwashing and damaging imagery at their fingertips.

I feel like we need to be having honest conversations when it comes to our relationship with food, and we should listen to ourselves if it's starting to spiral into something dangerous. If it is, it's time to get some help.

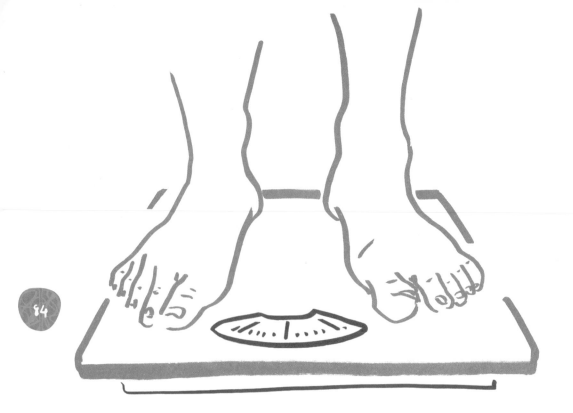

Concerned, I asked Susie Orbach, author of *Fat is a Feminist Issue*, *On Eating*, *Bodies* and *In Therapy* if she had noticed a change in women's attitudes towards their bodies over the years.

 I think the situation is so much worse," she said. "Every inch of our body, every aspect of our bodies has been commercialized, either by the beauty companies, the cosmetic surgery companies, the fashion houses, the food companies, the diet companies. So . . . the situation's much worse, much more unstable . . . The situation with our bodies is pretty serious. We're sort of supposed to have our body as our product rather than the place we live, and that's a really damaging concept.

The world of eating disorders is a complex **mess**. It's dizzying – it's panic-making. It is very trendy to seem in control of your diet. There are so many 'beautiful' people spearheading a bizarre and very money-driven revolution, all in the name of reclaiming our 'health' and 'loving' our bodies. Not all diets or eating plans are suspect, or dangerous, but many are encouraging obsessive behaviour around food. This can lead to eating disorders and send us spiralling out of control. Nutritionist Leo Pemberton says:

> I think one of the dangerous things . . . is that if you follow certain bloggers or Instagram stars, they will all have a slightly different ethos. So if you follow one person and they say, 'I think you should cut out meat, dairy and gluten,' then you also follow someone else and they say, 'You should cut out grains,' then that's where you start to cut out many more groups than those people themselves are cutting . . . If you're cutting out vitamins and minerals and things like calcium or protein from your diet — especially if you're still growing or you're very active — that's when it becomes dangerous and you can run into deficiencies and potentially an eating disorder, which you by no means set out for in the first place.

We all feel like that sometimes. But if it's lodged its way into your mind too firmly, it might be a problem you shouldn't be tackling alone. Eating disorders are very complex and sometimes aren't connected to our relationship with food at all, but perhaps to 'control' or 'self-harm', and sometimes it's a heady mix of all these and more. If you know deep down that things are spiralling, but don't know how to talk about it, a letter is always a good way of reaching out about your feelings and worries.

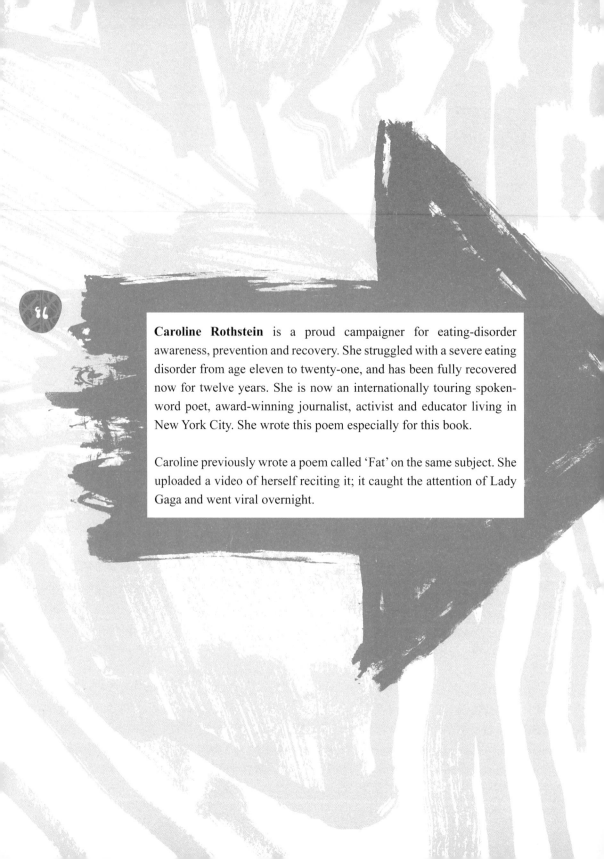

Caroline Rothstein is a proud campaigner for eating-disorder awareness, prevention and recovery. She struggled with a severe eating disorder from age eleven to twenty-one, and has been fully recovered now for twelve years. She is now an internationally touring spoken-word poet, award-winning journalist, activist and educator living in New York City. She wrote this poem especially for this book.

Caroline previously wrote a poem called 'Fat' on the same subject. She uploaded a video of herself reciting it; it caught the attention of Lady Gaga and went viral overnight.

FREE

by Caroline Rothstein

The time I told my eating disorder it could no longer live rent-free inside of me (the way it etched horror films into the lining of my oesophagus, the way it sacrificed my sanity on the altar of my throat, the way it tummy-tucked trauma into the residue of my fingernails and pierced grief on to the outskirts of my uvula, dangling with ache),

was a good day. It was a Thursday. November 18. Warm enough to forget I had ever seen the sun. Cold enough to forget my deepest secret – that I was enough. Loneliness seemed so sacred, what with the gapping crevices of shame that had atrophied my soul. Though this isn't about the ulcer, or the popped eye blood vessel, or the straight Cs, or

the red Solo plastic cups I filled with vomit like other people filled with beer at parties on weekends. This isn't about the suicidal thoughts, or the way I cut my wrist, and my thigh, and my forearm, and prayed that every day I might end up in the hospital so that someone might, in fact, see the pain that was eating me alive now breathing on my skin.

That is the obvious part, really. That is the textbook. That is the shit they make you read in health class when they tell you you're a statistic and make the bullies go home. That's the multi-billion-dollar diet industry that pleads for you to hate yourself so you'll forget the deepest secret – because it isn't just mine – see that's the stuff they'll tell you so that

it too can live rent-free underneath, inside, behind your skin. The time I told my eating disorder to find another home, I didn't want to die any more. I watched my dead brother float around my bedroom and tell me I had a body so wasn't it worth treating it like a temple? Wasn't it worth worshipping everything that lived within? He was there in the

room, my dead brother. And so was awe. And more than anything I saw my soul etched into the lining of my body, sacrificing my hysteria on the altar of my fear, the way it unhinged trauma from the residue of my fingernails and pierced faith into the outskirts of my uvula, dangling with trust. It was a good day when the all-knowing voice within

my stomach opened up into the depths of possibility. When I decided I was enough, and that my body was a triumph. And that resilience was the only prayer I'd ever need to sing. It was a good day when my heart wept for itself. When my brain reconnected with my soul. When the rent went up and recovery moved in and I finally had a tenant-free home.

97

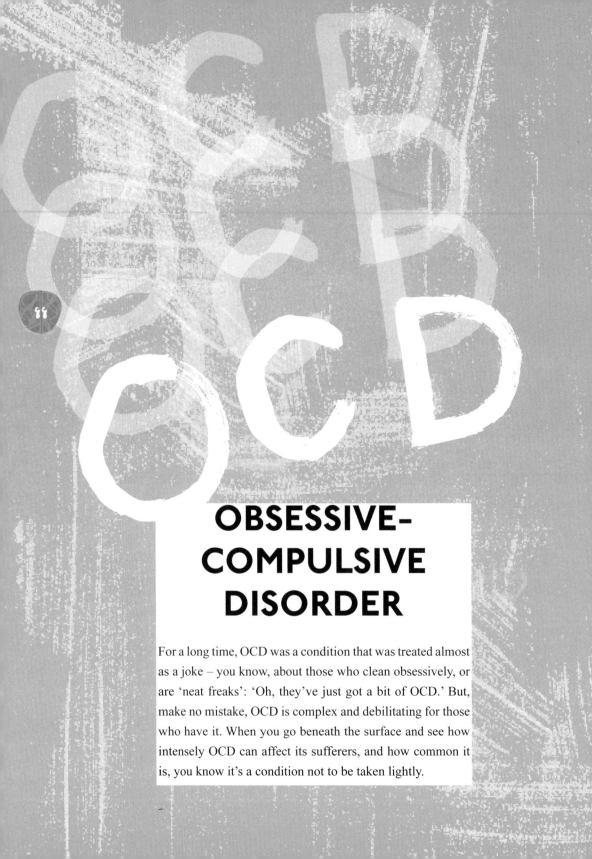

OBSESSIVE-COMPULSIVE DISORDER

For a long time, OCD was a condition that was treated almost as a joke – you know, about those who clean obsessively, or are 'neat freaks': 'Oh, they've just got a bit of OCD.' But, make no mistake, OCD is complex and debilitating for those who have it. When you go beneath the surface and see how intensely OCD can affect its sufferers, and how common it is, you know it's a condition not to be taken lightly.

" There are two main components to OCD, the obsessions and compulsions, but what combines the two is an intense feeling of anxiety.

In general, OCD sufferers experience obsessions that take the form of persistent and uncontrollable thoughts, images, impulses, worries, fears or doubts. They are often intrusive, unwanted, disturbing and significantly interfere with the ability to function on a day-to-day basis as they are incredibly difficult to ignore.

Compulsions are repetitive physical behaviours and actions or mental thought rituals that are performed over and over again in an attempt to relieve the anxiety caused by the obsessional thoughts. Avoidance of places or situations to prevent triggering these obsessive thoughts is also considered to be a compulsion. But, unfortunately, any relief that the compulsive behaviours provide is only temporary and short lived, and often reinforces the original obsession, creating a gradual worsening cycle of obsessions and compulsive behaviours.

Whilst the public perception of OCD is someone carrying out cleaning or checking compulsive ritualistic behaviours, the reality is that for many people obsessions and compulsions will be internal with no physical manifestation, an example is someone may be overly concerned with fears about sexuality or their relationship and will engage in lots of reassurance and checking, either with themselves or with loved ones.

It is fair to say that to some degree OCD-type symptoms are probably experienced at one time or another by most people. However, the key difference that segregates little quirks, often referred to by people as being 'a bit OCD' from the actual disorder is when the distressing and unwanted experience of obsessions and compulsions impacts to a significant level upon a person's everyday functioning — this represents a principal component in the clinical diagnosis of obsessive—compulsive disorder. "

"By my early twenties, I'd already spent half a decade trying to figure out the meaning of my relentless, graphic sexual thoughts. Maybe I was a self-loathing, homophobic lesbian who just couldn't accept who she was? Then one night, when I was high on antidepressants and Jägermeister, I saw two girls kissing at a house party. It was my light-bulb moment. These girls seemed so free and in love — a million light-years away. With my self-harm and my 24/7 flesh-crawling anxiety and my constant frightening mental images, I was on another planet. I sensed for the first time that I was mental, and googled the words 'intrusive thoughts', and my life changed forever."

Rose Bretécher, former sufferer of pure OCD , a type that includes obsessive, intrusive sexual thoughts. Rose is also the author of *Pure: A Memoir*, which recounts her experiences with and overcoming of OCD.

OCD: THE STATISTICS

- Around the world there are literally millions of people affected by OCD, and it is considered to be the fourth most common mental illness in many Western countries, and will affect men, women and children regardless of their race, religion, nationality or socio-economic group.

- Here in the United Kingdom, current estimates suggest that 1.2 per cent of the population will have OCD, which equates to twelve out of every 1,000 people, and based on the current estimates for the UK population, these statistics mean that, potentially, approximately 758,000 people are living with OCD at any one time.

- However, it is worth noting that a disproportionately high number, fifty per cent, of all these cases will fall into the severe category, with less than only a quarter being classed as mild cases. Which is why some estimates suggest that maybe two to three per cent of all those visiting their GP will be doing so because of OCD.

Stats provided by OCD UK

If any of this sounds familiar and you think that you're showing symptoms of OCD, you don't have to suffer in silence – there is treatment available. Go and see your GP and tell someone you trust about how you're feeling.

ADDICTION

When we think of addiction, we often think of alcohol, drugs or cigarettes, but actually an addiction is anything that you can't stop doing or stop thinking about – when you feel like you don't have control over its role in your life. Addiction can have a very serious effect on your mind, your body, your relationships and everything you do. People with more serious addictions often need professional intervention to help them break their damaging habits, and some addictions can even be life-threatening.

It is heartbreaking to watch someone lambast themselves for their addiction, while corroding their body, personality and relationships. And it shouldn't be underestimated how tightly an addiction can grip, and how hard it can be to escape it.

It is possible to be addicted to:

cigarettes   sex
illegal drugs   caffeine
Social media   exercise
prescribed drugs   alcohol
sugar   our phones   porn

COULD YOU BE ADDICTED?

If you are worried, try taking the test below.

Think about the thing you enjoy the most out of the list of possible addictions on the previous page and write it here:

○ ○

Do you . . . (circle your answer)

Crave it?	**YES / NO**
Do you feel relieved once you've used it or consumed it?	**YES / NO**
Do you feel irritable or angry if you are denied it, or try to withdraw from it?	**YES / NO**
Do you feel that you can't stop doing it?	**YES / NO**
Do you wish you did it less or not at all?	**YES / NO**

It is possible to overcome all forms of addiction if, deep in your gut, you are ready to confront it head on. Take a look at how you've answered the above. If you've circled YES three times or more, you may be at risk of addiction. There are organizations at the back of the book that can give you specific advice on what you can do about certain unhealthy addictions.

SELF-HARM

A bleak epidemic, sweeping silently over a generation. It is in the whispers of classrooms, wrenching guts in our tummies when we think of the things in this world that are hardest to understand.

WHY WE HURT OURSELVES

Here are some sad and scary statistics about self-harm:

- **One in twelve young people self-harm.**
- **Last year 38,000 young people were admitted to hospital because of their injuries through self-harming.**
- **Hospital admissions due to people self-harming increased by sixty-eight per cent in the last ten years.**

Self-harming is a response to anxiety, fear, chaos and trauma. For self-harmers, it is a coping mechanism and often a shameful secret. We need to deal with the shame factor first and foremost, TALK about self-harm and what lies behind it, and separate the fact from the fiction.

SELF-HARM: THE MYTHS

During my research for this book, I came across an awesome organization called selfharmUK. Their website is progressive, straight talking and easy to navigate. It lists the important **myths** and **misconceptions** surrounding self-harm, such as:

- It's only teenagers that self-harm.
- People who self-harm are attention-seeking.
- Only girls self-harm.
- Self-harm only involves cutting.
- Self-harm is easy to stop.
- Self-harm is a suicide attempt.
- Anyone who self-injures is crazy.
- Self-harm is a phase and something you just grow out of.
- People only self-harm if they've had a really sad life.

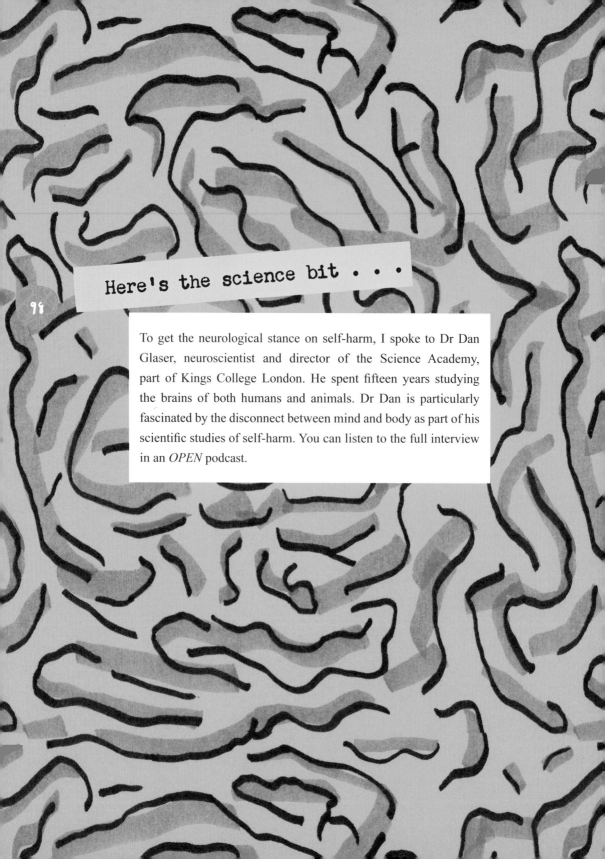

Here's the science bit . . . .

To get the neurological stance on self-harm, I spoke to Dr Dan Glaser, neuroscientist and director of the Science Academy, part of Kings College London. He spent fifteen years studying the brains of both humans and animals. Dr Dan is particularly fascinated by the disconnect between mind and body as part of his scientific studies of self-harm. You can listen to the full interview in an *OPEN* podcast.

"The first thing to say about it [self-harm] is that it is a paradoxical phenomenon, which is to say it's surprising. Why is it surprising? It's surprising because most of what our brains do, most of our biology, is about maintaining ourselves in good shape. So we sweat when we're hot, we get goose-bumps or shiver when we're cold. When we're thirsty — that's because the salts in our blood are telling our brain we need to drink.

Your whole system of pain in your body is largely designed to stop you from injuring yourself . . . So self-harm is a paradox from a logical point of view because it's an intentional or a deliberate act that goes against your own interests in biology."

GIRLS TALKING ABOUT
self-harm

As part of a short film project I was producing, I visited a school to talk to teenagers about self-harm. Here I was in the school library, a warm and comforting environment, full of potential.

It was during this hour-long discussion with these teenagers that I learnt more about the deep and lurking issue of self-harm amongst so many young people.

'Self-harm is everywhere.'

'In our year group at school, there's a lot of people that do it.'

'At least three in each class.'

'I feel it has a lot to do with peer pressure. I hear about one person doing it, and then I hear all their friends are doing it — a group is formed.'

'Why do you think people are drawn to do it?' I asked.

'Because they want to be popular.'

'A lot of people that do it are from broken homes.'

'So many people tell me they do it, and I don't know what to do.'

'So it's a trend?' I ask.

'Yeah. Just type the word "depressed" into Instagram.'

'I'm absolutely terrified at the moment, because of my little sister. She's ten. She's always having arguments with her friends, ya know. She's a complete drama queen, and I'm scared. I'm scared that she might feel the need to do it. If my sister did it, I just don't know what I would do — it's such a horrible thing. And to think that so many people do it. My sister could so easily feel depressed or give in to peer pressure or want to cut herself, because that's what so many people are doing. If this trend keeps going on, it's unavoidable . . .'

So, self-harm amongst teenagers is widespread. It's real and it's scary. But knowing that we are aware and talking about it more is heartening. We need to keep on talking.

SELF-HARM AND THE
ONLINE COMMUNITY

I decide to do some research. When I type certain triggering words into the search box on Instagram, a list of usernames floods my screen, all using the site to visually document their destructive journeys. All the aliases are a variation of each other, each flaunting the fact that they self-harm in their handles, some of which have a tagline labelled 'trigger warning'. I could see how compulsive it must be for some people, how 'catching' these online communities are. For vulnerable people, who desperately need validation, some kind of self-worth, the ease with which they can access the WRONG kind of support rather than portals of advice and help is frightening.

The fact is that self-harming hurts you, and anyone who encourages it is hurting you so much more.

I feel an overwhelming yearning for moderation online. I'm hoping that people know how to handle sites and social networks with care.

I will take this as another opportunity to say please be careful when you are feeling vulnerable. You do not need to be on every social networking site, all of the time. You know if a certain site or user profile is making you feel bad about yourself. It is time to click UNFOLLOW on the stuff that damages us: it feels very powerful and personally liberating to do so.

BE STRONG.

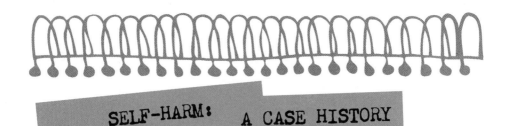

I interviewed a brave and beautiful woman – known here as 'A' for 'Anonymous' – who got in touch wanting to open up about her personal experiences with self-harm. Her journey is inspiring and real. You can listen to the podcast interview in full, but here are some powerful words.

A: I've struggled with self-harming since I was about thirteen – so a long, long time. I had a break, and a couple of years ago things started to get really bad. I had a breakdown, and it came back again. It really shocked me. I'm in my thirties and . . . it was like I was a teenager again, and I couldn't manage my feelings; I couldn't cope.

I remember looking for help on self-harm, and I think I was struggling to find anything that related to me at my age. Not just that – it's the shame around self-harm as well . . . It's something that even now I feel ashamed about and scared [to talk] about . . . There's a lot of embarrassment around it. It seems that it's such an extreme form of coping strategy . . . so traumatic and violent, that I couldn't imagine telling anyone what I've done to myself.

I remember scratching myself, and . . . I would cut myself with scissors or a knife, and that happened quite regularly. I was struggling a lot when I was younger, and I took an overdose as well when I'd just turned fourteen. I was just desperate, and after that I continued self-harming for a long, long time. But no one – apart from friends that knew about it – no one really picked up on it. They could see it . . .

G: And were there specific things in your life that you were particularly upset about, or was it a more amalgamated mix of dealing with general life and growing up?

A: Yeah, I lost my dad when I was really, really young, when I was seven, and . . . that was really difficult . . . On top of being a teenager, fancying boys, being conscious of my body, that was a huge thing. I remember when I was . . . about eight or nine, and looking at myself and thinking, 'If only my legs were smaller.' So it was just this whole mix of growing up as well as what had happened to us as a family . . . If I'd have known, I think, as a teenager, why it was happening, why I was doing it to myself, I think I'd have been able to find ways to cope with things better, and it would've stopped earlier, and I wouldn't have hurt myself so much . . . [If] we share experiences . . . there is a way to kind of deal with it, or to manage it, to get better from it . . . speaking to others and professionals will really help, it will . . .

The feelings still come, and I've got a better way of coping . . . This sounds silly, but I've been trying to make amends with my body. I have scars on my body and they are a constant reminder of times in my life where I've felt completely lost and . . . desperate. But I have to kind of accept my body now and make amends with it . . . I'm . . . now starting my life finally.

G: **If you had any tips for anyone, regardless of age – whether they are thirteen or thirty-four – and they can connect with some of the stories that you've told, what would they be?**

A: I think the most important thing for me was to talk to people, and to talk to the right people as well – seek professional help. There are so many organizations out there – I got referred to a clinic. They gave me a list of numbers that you can call. I called every one when I was desperate . . .

G: **Have you got any recommendations?**

A: I spoke to SANE, and there were support groups that I attended. And that was my biggest help, because it was through that that I found out there were a lot of people with eating disorders who self-harmed as a part of that. There's various groups and organizations.

G: **It's impossible to be completely sure, but, in your opinion, do you think you would have returned to harming if you'd accessed the right help for you when you were harming when younger?**

A: I truly believe if I'd had access to it when younger, hurting myself would not have been a coping strategy for me when I was older. There is help available. To anyone out there struggling with self-harm or emotional issues, you deserve support, you deserve love. Because of the help I received, I survived self-harm, and so will you. So can you. You are not alone. That is the most important thing to remember. You are not alone.

G: **OK. Thank you for sharing so much. Thank you, thank you, thank you . . .**

SELF-HARM:
GETTING BETTER

We're beginning to understand that, as well as practising caution online, talking about self-harm and exploring the feelings behind it are hugely important in overcoming it. Our feelings and our despair can be overwhelming, but try not to let it create a fog that surrounds you – give yourself time to take a deep breath and consider how to face the issue with perspective rather than harm. Tomorrow is a new day and you are so beautifully precious. Speak up, speak out and be kind to yourself. So many people want you to live a full life and want to help guide you to be happy even if it doesn't always feel like it. I for one am one of those people. So don't be ashamed. If you are self-harming or thinking about it – tell someone immediately and learn to shift the act of self-harm to one of self-care.

MISSION STATEMENT

Dear Top Dogs of social media companies and the government,

It is time. It is time to take a stand. It is time to spend a portion of the money generated from tech innovation on 'tech protection'. I urge you to please accept responsibility for protecting those young, vulnerable and mentally fragile users of your sites by proactively filtering potentially damaging imagery and monitoring submissions to online forums, which are steeped in negative body imagery and promote body harm.

I worry for the young and inquisitive minds, and in my research I realized all too quickly that there isn't enough counterbalance in terms of practical advice and anti-self-harming, body-loathing information. Could there be a strategy put in place? A clearer system that goes beyond the 'report' button? A campaign to explain what you do to protect your users? An in-house 'positivity squad' — monitoring activity of the most harmful sites and users?

Rather than focusing energy on yanking down any picture of a woman's nipples or any sign of menstrual blood — I shout from the rooftops that it is the romanticization of self-harm as a trend that needs to be tackled. It requires boldness and commitment from those in a position of authority to enforce change. We need help and a sense of responsibility alongside these powerful and alluring and often brilliant sites, networks and campaigns.

This needs to be on the agenda — something needs to be done to protect the well-being and mental health of those who spend most of their social life online. The future of tech and social networking needs to be about social consciousness and empowerment, rather than the rampant sense of 'anything goes', which exacerbates bad mental health, creating an epidemic of self-loathing.

It feels like it's become too difficult to tackle, too dark to raise, too scary to mention — but there really is an epidemic amongst young people, and it's time to do something about it.

Yours sincerely,

Gemma Cairney

Gemma Cairney

Cut out and send to local MPs and those in a position of power.

IT'S NOT YOUR FAULT –
STOP BEATING YOURSELF UP

For those who feel bad about not feeling OK...

We ALL mess up some-times

We ALL HAVE a DARK SIDE

and sometimes feel in the shade.

109

WE ALL CARRY GUILT AND SHAME SOMETIMES

110

I HATE MYSELF. Woe WHY DID I DO SORRY THAT?

How we deal with our dark sides or recover from messing up is the IMPORTANT ISSUE. It is time to stop beating ourselves up for the way we feel and instead OPEN up about our feelings.

You know when you wear a new wool jumper, and you are wishing you'd worn a T-shirt underneath it – but you've realized too late, and you've already stepped out of the house? And it's itching and scratching your bare skin? Making you feel like you're trapped in your own jumper? Making you want to squirm and break free? Guilt and shame can cause your soul to itch in the same way – embedding themselves in your brain in a way that'll make you feel like the jumper can never be taken off.

I think as a society we are excellent at feeling bad about ourselves, obsessing over our worst qualities, when most of us are actually pretty decent human examples. The number of 'guilt-free' products out there implies we should be feeling guilty for everything we usually do. Life is too short to feel guilty about eating cake, that's for sure.

It is worth assessing how often you feel guilt or shame, and whether it balances out with feeling in control and neutral. Work out your patterns of bad feelings – you will either realize how ridiculous it is to apply them to certain things, or accept that if you are doing something that's making you feel genuinely negative, then you need to find some ways to stop doing it.

YOU ARE NOT
alone

The worst thing about feeling down is how lonely and isolated it can make you feel. YOU ARE NOT ALONE. This book and everyone involved in it have unshockable souls – we believe it is never too late, and there are lots of brilliant things for everyone out there. If you are feeling out of control, I urge you to take steps to speak to someone who is trained in hearing your tale. You are not the only one who has felt this way. The sad truth is that many, many others do too. We're gonna have to work together on collectively achieving better mental health in the modern world.

Together, we can be happy and strong.

The
A to Z
of a Happy Mind

Here is a list of things to try that might pull you out of a dark place. Different things work for different people, so here is a whole alphabet of practical tools, therapy techniques and emotional concepts to consider en route to feeling good in your mind.

Advice – get some. There's a list of places you can go for confidential, practical help at the back of this book. **Ashamed:** don't be. **Ask** for help.

Ambient music. For some, music can relieve the symptoms of panic. There are albums and albums' worth of ambient music that can literally transcend the most fraught of minds.

Breaking bad thought patterns. Do you notice the same things coming into your head all the time? Notice these things, write them down, then think of a positive thought to replace them with.

Crying isn't weak or pathetic – it can help you work through your emotions.

Creativity can make you feel better – making some art or writing a poem about how you feel can help. You're not alone.

Communities exist online for almost anything you're going through – find your people. **Choices:** you have them – even if you feel helpless. **CBT**, or cognitive behavioural therapy, is a brilliant and very popular form of talking therapy that's designed to change our patterns of thought and help us understand why we feel certain things sometimes.

Counselling is widely available for free through your GP, and sometimes talking to someone impartial might be what you need. **Chemical imbalance** in your brain might be what's making you feel depressed. If so, medication might help, and there's nothing wrong with that.

Distractions can help you get out of your head – find some happy ones. Going to see a doctor can often be a good place to start, to make sure there are no underlying health issues that are affecting your state of mind, and a **diagnosis** might make you see things more clearly. There's NOTHING you can tell them that they won't have heard before.

Endorphins. OH YES. I love them. Make them your best friends, sourced the natural way. Stimulate endorphins by moving your body, doing some cartwheels in an open space. Produced by the central nervous system and the pituitary gland, endorphins are essentially happy-makers in our brain.

Educate yourself. Seek out information on the way you're feeling.

F **Friends and family** – hopefully, amongst them there will be at least one person who will get what you're going through and be able to help. Have a think about who that might be, and arrange to talk to them.

G **Get out of the house.** It might be tempting to hide under your duvet until the end of time, and sometimes it might even make you feel a bit better. But, eventually, you have to get out in the world. It's not so bad.

H **Healthy habits** and eating. If your mind is a bit unhealthy, then try to keep your body healthy while you work the rest of it out.

Help others. This is all about thinking about someone else rather than yourself. When you're feeling bad, it's easy to forget that other people might be worse off than you are.

I **Imagination.** Think about the people, places and things that make you happy, and imagine them when you're feeling low.

J **Joy.** Find it. Channel it. Remember it.

K **Kindness.** Go easy on yourself, above all. Stop punishing yourself for not getting it right all the time. Remember kindness towards other people: an embrace with a friend, a smile at a stranger. Asking someone if they are all right when they have a face full of pain. Kindness is the warmest feeling.

L **Laughing** also releases endorphins, and you should do it whenever you can. **Laugh long, laugh loud, laugh often.** A good giddy giggle has been shown to reduce stress hormones. There is even such a thing as laughter therapy. **Laughter therapy** has been shown to have beneficial effects on various aspects of biochemistry. When laughing, the brain releases endorphins that can also relieve physical pain.

M **Medication.** There's no stigma in taking it, if it's what's right for you.

Mindfulness is a totally free way of finding some peace in your brain and living in the moment. Check out the Headspace app for how to do it.

Music can have a powerful effect on your mood – make some happy playlists for when you need a boost.

Nourish your soul and your body; listen to their **needs**. Say **no** to anyone who is dragging you down rather than lifting you up.

One thing at a time! Identify anything that is making you feel bad, make a list and tick them off.

Pets are proven to make us happy.

Positivity is SO important. List three things every day that made you feel good, however small. Have **patience** with yourself. Some things take time, and everyone moves at their own pace.

Psychologists are best placed to deal with certain problems, and your GP will be able to refer you if they think you would benefit from talking to one.

Quiet – find somewhere peaceful. If you're an introvert, you might need to take some time alone to feel better. Get away from the noise of the world – that includes social media! Ask **questions** – if you see a GP, a counsellor or any other trained professional, write down anything you want to know and go through it with them. They are there to answer any questions you might have.

Read – reading books is the most enriching escapism there is.

Relax in the best way you know how. Whether it's watching TV, reading, having a bath, gardening or hanging out with your friends – do it regularly. Let your shoulders drop, breathe deeply and relax.

Reflect – don't always look ahead, but breathe deep in the present, and reflect on the past.

Support – can be found in the right places.

Space – make some in your brain.

Smell. I love the idea that fragrance and aromatherapy can be a 'go-to' for a busy mind. Bergamot and eucalyptus are advised for 'emotional exhaustion', for example, as is ginger for 'intellectual fatigue'. A fantastic book about this, and more, is *The Fragrant Mind: Aromatherapy for Personality, Mind and Emotion* by Valerie Ann Worwood, 1996.

Talk about it, **tell** someone, seek **therapy**.

Understand your triggers.

Vent. Shout and scream if you need to, to someone who understands you.

Walk it out and **write** it down – take time and space with your thoughts, and they might sort themselves into some sort of order you can understand.

XOXO. Kissing the right person can make you feel more rooted to the planet than anything you can do with another human being.

Yoga. Get bendy and feel more in control of your body.

Zzzzzz . . . get enough sleep! Sleep is soul power.

READING LIST FOR MENTAL HEALTH

Some great, inspirational books that deal with mental health are listed below.

She's Come Undone by Wally Lamb

Mind Your Head by Juno Dawson

Undone by Cat Clarke

Mealtimes and Milestones: A Teenager's Diary of Moving on from Anorexia
by Constance Barter

Understanding Teenage Depression
by Maureen Empfield

The Brain – The Story of You
by David Eagleman

YOUR BODY
† SOUL

INTRODUCTION

Our BODIES – the ships that carry our cargo of thoughts, feelings, loves and anxieties through the world. Alive and kicking. Even though they are amazing machines, we often find it all too easy to be at war with our bodies, or feel trapped inside them. In this part of the book, we will explore how this can happen, and assess how it might be possible to love our bodies more. Because they are all – without exception – REMARKABLE.

Your body is an extraordinary, living, breathing, fantastical mass of cells, which people spend years and years studying to understand. Your body can do so many amazing things. It can even heal itself. Isn't that mind-blowing?

Our SOULS. Imagine an immensely deep, glistening wishing well – the type of well you can imagine spouting a rainbow. Our souls are OUR wells: the core of who we really are. Our soul is our personality, our feeling-holder, our gut instinct, our individual spirit, the part of us that makes us feel happy and alive. The best thing about souls is that there are no two the same. Your soul is wholly unique to you. It burns bright, with all the colours of the warmest flames. Our body and soul are so interconnected they blur and work together as one. In order to nurture our souls, we need to learn to love and understand our bodies.

With all this in mind, how do you feel in your soul about the way your body actually looks? Go and stand naked in front of a mirror. Are you aware of how wonderful its individualities are? Do you know its every crease? How have you felt about your body over the years? Has it changed? Do you remember finding your first pubes? (I recall the day I spent staring in disbelief at mine . . . I just couldn't believe that my body had grown such thick, curly black hair . . . down there.)

Then there is that defiant hair sprouting from your nipple . . . which keeps coming back, no matter how many times you pluck it out. (Yes – that can happen anywhere between your teens and your twenties and is completely NORMAL, so don't let anyone make you feel it isn't.) Pubes, creases, breasts and hips – they all appear just when you're feeling at your most self-conscious, and it can feel weird and uncomfortable. It's very easy to start scrutinizing and criticizing bits of yourself that are in fact bloody marvellous.

I'm in knee deep

For a flicker of time, I remember being absolutely infuriated by my knees. OK, so let me try to explain. Being mixed race means there are some parts of your body that are darker, more 'black', than others. In the gene pool, these things could have swung either way, but my knees are darker than the rest of my legs, and I also scar more easily. That is the way darker-pigmented skin is. A boyfriend once tactlessly asked me why I had what looked like 'muddy knees' in comparison to the rest of my body. I remember this getting me down, and I really disliked my knees for a bit. On reflection, I find this fact so ridiculous that I am almost ashamed to put it in this book. MY KNEES. I HAD A PROBLEM WITH MY KNEES. That boy didn't mean to be unkind, but it was kinda HIS problem, not MINE. Of course, my hang-ups didn't start and end there – but this is up there with the most ludicrous tripe I have ever thought about myself . . . and, trust me, there has been a LOT of ludicrous tripe along the way.

A LITTLE JOURNEY THROUGH MY PERSONAL BODY-RESENTMENT TIMELINE

During my teens, I desperately wanted bigger boobs, and relentlessly eyeballed the money-making bullcrap of supposedly 'herbal' pills that promised to 'miraculously' and 'completely naturally' increase their size. What a load of money-making codswallop. I used to stand so close to the mirror that I convinced myself the hair on my top lip was actually going to get in the way of my life, that I was a freak of nature – never taking into consideration the fact that I was practically KISSING the mirror. If anyone was to ever get that close to my face, they'd probably have their eyes closed . . . COS THAT'S WHAT YOU DO TO SMOOCH for gyaaaad's sake.

I also had spots bad enough to be called acne. My entire forehead was decorated with pus-filled volcanoes; I wore ashy, fudge-brown foundation in an attempt to cover them up, which was often two or three shades too light – as back then (and still now) many high street, affordable make-up brands didn't have the right shades for my skin tone (they weren't stock priority for a town called Horsham in West Sussex, where I was one of only two black people at my school).

As an adult, I have harboured a deep desire for a tummy that doesn't protrude so much that people occasionally mistake its pokey-outness for pregnancy. (My tummy actually protrudes because I have a fibroid – a benign lump of useless muscle in my tummy – which would require the hassle of serious surgery to remove, and that I've been advised not to do if it doesn't cause me any trouble – which it doesn't right now.)

The times my confidence has been most challenged have all been to do with my career. When I landed my first job as a presenter in the outer space that my industry can sometimes represent, I found myself surrounded by people trying really hard to be a 'celebrity'. Despite the idea of being famous rendering me a flinching, gagging mess – there are certain dizzyingly glamorous elements of my job that are too fun to ignore. Like going to the Brit Awards, or sitting in the front row at a fashion show, or going to a party too swanker-dank-danky to turn down. There are those events where I am hardened by champagne promises and the plumes of a silent visual hierarchy cos the place is filled with pedigree-cat-like people who are so shiny that your jaw drops when you are near them. Women whose bodies are so waif-like you want to swaddle them in a blanket and feed them like you would if you found a small bird.

So, yeah, I've wondered before whether it'd be worth changing my lifestyle: losing the freedom I enjoy from indulging in all types of food, exercising as a priority over a lie-in, or getting on with some work – or starting my own production company or writing or pitching radio documentaries – instead of meeting a friend I love for a drink and chat. But that JUST AIN'T ME. A me that tried to fit into a 'celebrity' mould would mean a very unhappy me.

After nearly a decade of working in a job that means I am occasionally in the public eye, I have received abuse on Twitter for 'not being able to talk properly', and for the colour of my skin, and, worse still, been told by a production company that I'm not 'girly' enough to even screen-test for a job I'm experienced enough to do.

All things considered, I feel unbelievably lucky to have grown up without the everyday annoyances and insecurities I have about my body (or the things other people have said to me about my body) ever causing me to drift into unhealthy territory. I don't know if it is because I was a teen before Instagram and selfie culture, but I was blissfully unaware of the size of my body in comparison to others. I never felt fat or thin; I didn't talk about weight with my friends. Without the constant sharing of photographs in the public arena, without the invitation to judge our bodies given to every stranger on the internet, my friends and I were able to happily exist without comparing ourselves to other women.

Don't get me wrong, 'body dysmorphia' – a term used for a corrupted sense of the shape or size of your body – has always existed, but now more than ever it seems that this negative relationship with our bodies has become almost acceptable . . . normal, even.

I thoroughly err on the 'f*ck it' side of life. I love my body, its caramel colour, and its willingness to dance and wiggle to all music. I love my boobs (which grew in the end, to two perfectly round jam-doughnut-sized jigglers). I love that these legs have walked me up the 5,188 metres of Mount Kenya, cycled me from London to Paris, jumped me into the sea where I live. I love my face and its mixed-racedness, the unpredictability of my tightly coiled afro hair. My body is me. My body is a punk that will be clothed in whatever I'm in the mood for. I have not been on the front of magazines, like some of the TEENY TINY crew. I do not fit into the cookie cutter of the who's who of the famous and cool. But I am happy. And that makes me lucky.

What WORRIES me is that now I feel like I'm constantly hearing from people dealing with deep-rooted feelings of hate for their bodies, leading to obsessive dieting, cosmetic surgery or self-harm. If you are feeling a sadness towards your body, you are definitely not alone. I hope that reading about it will help you feel like you can talk about and explore all these feelings and start loving your body.

The feeling of not looking right is backed up by magazine covers, Insta-followers, the sense that SKINNY = better. I can see why and how this affects our sense that our own bodies aren't right. Celebrity is a simmering pot of false truths when it comes to representing life. If you entertain the celebrity lifestyle as aspirational, it is near impossible not to be sucked into thinking you have to be a certain type of skinny and play the game by representing yourself in a certain way to be accepted.

123

Please, BE KIND to yourself and to others: it will pour into your smile. It'll make you dazzle, glisten and shine. A smile is what should be promoted on EVERYTHING. A true smile is sexier, cooler, more aspirational than any thigh gap on the planet.

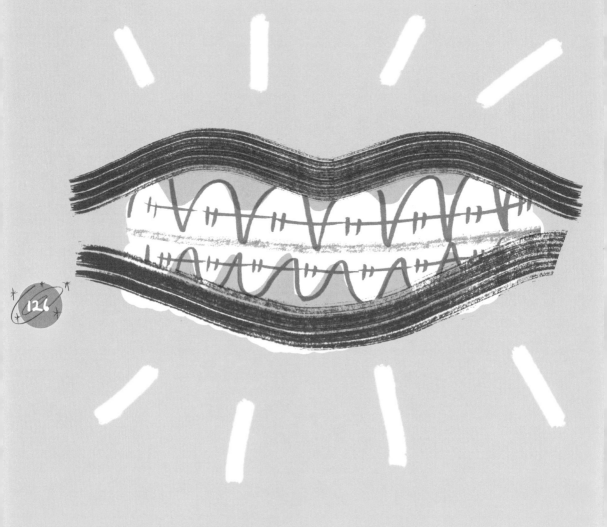

126

YOUR REMARKABLE BODY

The first step towards loving your body is understanding how special it is. Our bodies are as remarkable as we are fragile, and it's time to celebrate, explore and enjoy our bodies while we can.

I talked to the incredible Professor Hugh Montgomery, a man who knows a lot about bodies.

He's not only the director of the Institute for Human Health and Performance at University College London, but he also holds the world record for underwater piano playing!

I asked him some questions in a mission to discover just how magnificent human bodies are.

Tell us something we don't know about a part of the body.

The heart isn't just a pump. It is FOUR pumps joined together, with its own electrical wiring system. It pumps enough blood to fill an Olympic swimming pool every year.

Is it true that many people reading this will live to over one hundred?

Yes. Life expectancy has been rising steadily in the last half-century or more, and many now live to one hundred. When I was a junior doctor back in 1990, anyone over the age of sixty-five went to the 'geriatric' team. None of us would class someone of sixty-five as 'old' any more!

If we were to have a party to celebrate the human body, and I asked everyone to come dressed as their favourite body part, which would you come as and why?

That's hard. I guess coming dressed as a muscle would be hard. But the joy of being able to exercise – run, jump, dance – depends on good muscles, bones and joints. Likewise, the brain brings the joy of consideration, problem-solving and more. But every organ is truly remarkable – and one doesn't have to look very hard to see that.

WOW. You're feeling quite impressed with your body now, aren't you? Good, because it is a simply incredible, messy, pulsating, super-smart machine.

PERIODS

At some point during puberty, a girl's body starts preparing itself for egg fertilization, and this happens EVERY SINGLE MONTH, for decades. The uterus is quite the relentless queen in her mission to get a fertilized egg. Its lining gets thicker every monthly cycle, essentially in preparation for pregnancy. If no fertilized egg ends up there, which (among other reasons) happens when the egg does not meet a viable sperm, the uterus lining is shed through the vagina. This process is officially known as MENSTRUATION, more commonly known as having a PERIOD.

THE BLOODY NUMBERS

On average, each of those born female will have around 480 periods in their life.

A ballpark of 334 million of the world's population are having their periods right now.

Periods last anything from 2 to 7 days.

The average menstruator spends thousands on disposable products, and throws away 11,000 pads or tampons into landfills throughout their reproductive lifetime.

One egg is released from a woman's body 12 to 14 days after an actual period, during the time that is known as ovulation.

On average, 2.4 tablespoons of actual blood is lost during the menstrual cycle, and a further 1 to 6 tablespoons of menstrual fluid.

(Don't know about you, but it often feels like enough to fill six 2-litre cola bottles to me!)

Until the year 2000, tampons incurred a 17.5 per cent tax in the UK.

If you are a trans guy or a proud uterus owner who identifies as non-binary, genderfluid or agender, check out page 146, which talks about including menstruators of all genders.

In Burkina Faso, 83 per cent of girls have nowhere to change their sanitary menstrual materials (source: Unicef).

The average menstrual cycle may be longer or shorter than 28 days - anywhere from 21 to 35 is pretty normal!

(Anyone else worry they were pregnant on day 29 just because you hadn't got your period yet? Just me?!!!) If you want to know what the average is for you, chart your cycle! Use your phone calendar, diary, or one of a zillion apps out there. Clue is a great app because it's not sponsored by a tampon company trying to grab your cash. It gives you a place to record loads of cool stats, it's nicely designed and it's not so pink and stereotypically girly that you'll want to vom!

AND SO. IT'S HAPPENING. Periods are a THING, but NO ONE EVER TALKS ABOUT THEM. Rather than create embarrassment, let's turn it into wonderment – periods are part of the whole business of creating human life, after all. V. COOL.

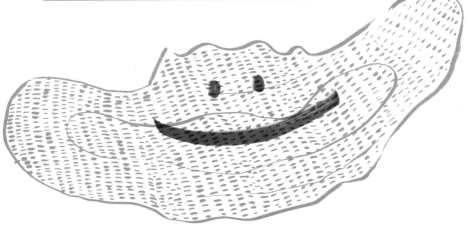

We all experience menstruation differently – for some, periods are light and pain-free; for others, they are heavier and cause cramping and bloating. Occasionally periods can be made very painful and last longer than normal because of underlying conditions such as endometriosis. If you are suffering badly and for longer than is normal, please talk to your parent or guardian and your doctor. It is very unlikely there is something seriously wrong, but by talking about it you will get the help you need to get through your period.

Periods are the great female equalizer, and practically everyone has an embarrassing period tale. I think that by sharing our stories we can lose the dread that comes with the prospect of a leak. It's crap if it happens to you, but remember that you're not alone! Here's my story . . .

THE WORST LEAK OF MY LIFE

I started my periods when I was twelve, and I'll never forget having to use the staff loos at school to change my sanitary towel for the first time. On that note, why are they called that? 'Sanitary towel' sounds so clinical. SO embarrassing. That's exactly how periods are marketed, isn't it? All the packaging – way too PINK, vagina-shaming and EMBARRASSING . . . Anyway, over the subsequent years, I thought I had got a grip on the monthly blood-fest. On the advice of my mum, I had 'graduated' to tampons. I was a period 'pro', head held high in the air. Granted, the pains were like a war in my womb and made me vomit – but I was holding it down, this period malarkey.

Fast-forward to me aged seventeen at a birthday party. I was twisting and shouting

the night away, at a party – beneath rainbow disco lights, lost in a cloud of R'n'B and twirly good times – with the boyfriend who made my heart pound harder than anyone had before. I was on fire. I had on my dream dress: it was from Tammy (a shop that was the bee's knees for teens everywhere in the nineties and early noughties – a bit like Topshop is today). It was a reversible satin dress with bra-like straps instead of normal ones – all adjustable and suggestive. This dress was SO good, stretchy satin, clingy, classy – AND, as it was reversible, either burgundy or black; I'd gone for chic black. A safe option, as I was on my period and I wouldn't have to fear leaking.

Anyway, there I was in my Tammy dress feeling damned fine and period-pain free. Everything felt so good, so unlimited. We danced till closing, around midnight. We were not in the mood for this night to end. How could it? It was fun of the best type. There I was perched on my boyfriend's lap, holding court amongst a rabble of lads, booming with laughter and sweat . . . till the lights came on, and the cheesiest of cheese DJs announced on the mic that it was time to leave. The party was over, and it was time for everyone to stop chasing dreams and go home. We didn't want to, but we pushed out giggles to the ultimate maximum, and then . . .

Then I stood up, removed myself from my boyfriend's lap, glanced down and saw the equivalent of all my nightmares coming true. There on my beloved's lap, on his off-white chinos, was a distinct puddle of BLOOD. I had leaked period blood, but had been too sweaty and happy to notice before. Worse still, the lights were up bright – as bright could be – and EVERYONE could see, staring in disbelief at the red stain on my boy's trousers. My eyes were hot with tears. I was a husk, my self-confidence blown away in a matter of seconds. My eyes met my boyfriend's, desperate for security and a sign of hope. I couldn't speak: embarrassment had rendered me speechless.

'Hahahahahahahhahahahahahaha,' squealed my friend Miriam. 'If you'd rubbed the other way, you'd have made the perfect England flag.'

It goes without saying that my boyfriend was not pleased. Beat that for the worst leak of your life.

See, MANY of us have been victims of the unexpected gush of the messy period. Many of us have been caught unawares by a sudden blood waterfall at the most inconvenient time and wearing the most inappropriate clothes. Periods are often cheeky and unpredictable. But if it happens to you, it's not the end of the world. One day you'll look back on it and laugh!

Tips + tales from da gals

'Please make sure you tell everyone not to wear a sanitary towel and go swimming,' said one of my mates when I asked her about a period she'd rather forget. 'I put two sanitary towels in my swimming costume to protect me from any leakage . . . only to find that, once I'd gone down the first water slide, they'd BOTH inflated in between my legs to the size of a small arm-band in my crotch. I literally had to put my hands in front of the bulge and run to the toilet to sort it out.'

'The worst is when you go to another country and you have come on, and you're, like, Where are the tampons? Where am I? What's going on? AND it's, like, twenty minutes before I'm going on live TV. And you're, like, Arrrrrghhhhh. I'm leaking through my fishnets!' – Marawa the Amazing, world-famous hula-hooper (more from her on pages 300–302).

Feel free to write or draw your depiction of THE WORST LEAK YOU'VE EVER HAD. It might feel good to get it down. Go into as much or as little detail as you want.

IF YOU'RE A BOY AND WANT TO KNOW MORE ABOUT PERIODS, HERE ARE SOME DOS AND DON'TS

 find out about the menstrual cycle and how it works.

 ask your school to include boys in lessons on periods – and if there are no lessons, demand them!

 find out about the different types of menstruation management (tampons, etc.) so you can get used to them if a friend or family member wants you to buy or borrow some for them.

 squirm at any sign of period paraphernalia. If a girl leaves a tampon wrapper on the side in the bathroom, or whatever – give her a break. There's quite a lot of fiddling around that's involved in a period.

 tease someone if they leak blood through their clothes (or on your clothes!) – play it cool and help them out.

 assume someone is 'on their period' if they are in a bad mood with you. It's more likely you've wound them up all by yourself, and mentioning periods will NOT do you any favours.

 135

 assume that if someone's on their period they can't get pregnant – you can get pregnant if you're ovulating, and some people ovulate more than once in a month every now and then!

If you are feeling a bit like you can't talk about your period to anybody and you are often grossed out by it, it's time to work out how to navigate your way through this biologically brilliant but messy time of the month. How chilled are you about the blob? (Yes, that is possibly the world's WORST way to describe it. That and 'on the red'. Though my favourite has got to be 'surfing the crimson wave', thanks to the legendary film *Clueless*, which, if you haven't watched it – YOU MUST!)

PMT

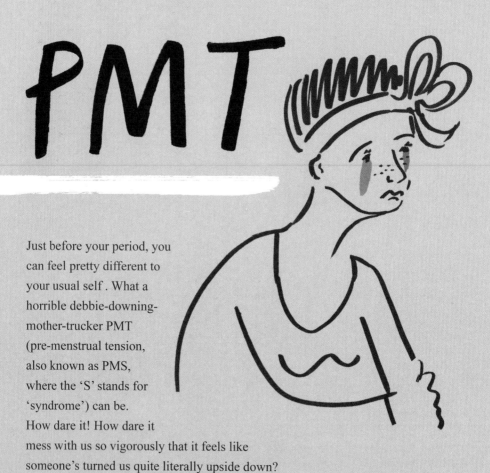

Just before your period, you can feel pretty different to your usual self . What a horrible debbie-downing-mother-trucker PMT (pre-menstrual tension, also known as PMS, where the 'S' stands for 'syndrome') can be. How dare it! How dare it mess with us so vigorously that it feels like someone's turned us quite literally upside down?

Mood swings? For some, it's more like a 'mood tsunami'. One of the most annoying things about PMT is how easy it is to forget about it once a period is all over. Once the crimson tide has been surfed, your body forgets the pain and the emotional rawness as quickly as it was knocked for six in the first place. For most of us, we just have to get used to it, know it's going to come and accept that it probably won't last very long. If, however, your PMT is lasting longer than two weeks and starting to really get you down, talk to your doctor about it. It's a natural companion to periods – before and during – but it is always good to get some expert advice if you're worried.

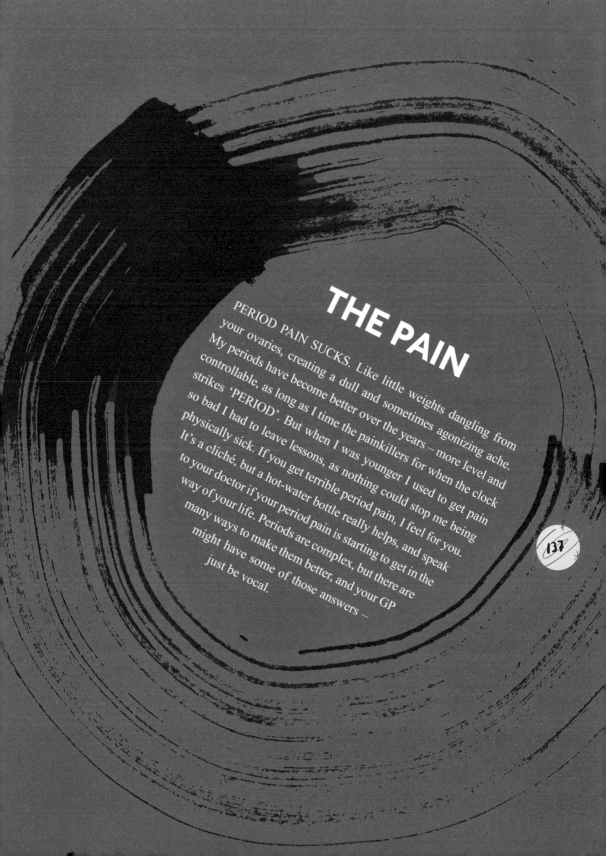

THE PAIN

PERIOD PAIN SUCKS. Like little weights dangling from your ovaries, creating a dull and sometimes agonizing ache. My periods have become better over the years – more level and controllable, as long as I time the painkillers for when the clock strikes 'PERIOD'. But when I was younger I used to get pain so bad I had to leave lessons, as nothing could stop me being physically sick. If you get terrible period pain, I feel for you. It's a cliché, but a hot-water bottle really helps, and speak to your doctor if your period pain is starting to get in the way of your life. Periods are complex, but there are many ways to make them better, and your GP might have some of those answers – just be vocal.

137

PERIOD QUIZ, ANYONE?

When buying menstrual products, do you:

A Either use reusables and tell your friends all about them, or boldly festoon the checkout till with your monthly supply of sanitary products, proud as punch, and don't ask for a bag to hide them in?

B Feel flushed and agitated, but know that it's essential and a fact of life?

C Get your mum, sister or even your dad to do it because you cannot bear to buy them yourself?

You get bad cramps every month – how do you deal with it?

A It's awful, but you've spoken to lots of people around you about how it affects you specifically, so everybody can try to understand when it's at its worst.

B You stock up on pain relief, put a brave face on it and only complain to your closest mates.

C You don't tell a soul, even if it really hurts, because you would rather die than let anyone know you are on your period. You hope nothing worse is wrong, but are afraid to mention it to your doctor.

When heading to the loo during your time of the month, you:

A Are happy to openly grab a tampon or pad out of your bag, and see no shame in anyone seeing it in your hand as you stroll on over.

B Furtively stuff your tampon or pad up your sleeve.

C Have a special discreet pouch in your bag for disguising your menstrual products so it looks like you're going to put make-up on.

What is a Mooncup?

A A brand name for a menstrual cup – a reusable alternative to tampons or sanitary towels/pads, which is made of a small silicone cup that is inserted into your vagina.

B A barometer that looks a bit like a dreamcatcher, used by hippies to judge when a period is due according to the alignment of the stars.

C A red mug with a moon picture on it.

You're worried you've leaked all over your light jeans at a barbecue. What do you do?

A Ask the mates you are sitting with to check as you stand up and to holler 'CODE RED' if it's happened.

B Wrap your jacket round your waist, stand up really quickly and scuttle to the loo to check.

C Disregard this question, as you only wear black during your period.

In a bid to raise awareness for women around the world who have no access to feminine hygiene products, Kiran Gandhi made the headlines when she ran the London Marathon in 2015. What did she do?

A Free bleeding (meaning she was on her period and ran without protection).

B Dressed up as a tampon.

C You don't even wanna know if it's got ANYTHING to do with periods.

When asked why she appeared ill after a race at the Olympics in Rio 2016, Fu Yuanhui, the bronze-medal-winning Olympic swimmer from China, said in an interview that her stomach pain was due to:

A Menstrual cramps, which made her tired after her race, although she said it was not an excuse.

B Swimming in a white suit and swim cap with a string attached, to protest the lack of tampon use in China.

C You don't want to know, and hope it has nothing to do with periods because, eww.

Mostly As: The Magnificent Menstruator

GURL, you are owning menstruation. You are fearless, have embraced your monthly cycle and realize that communication and expressiveness when it comes to periods is a healthy thing. You may be interested in the 'Period Activism' movements emerging online.

Mostly Bs: The Period Tolerater

You are the most common type of menstruator. You are aware and accept the fact that you have a period once a month – though you still find it an embarrassing fact of the female condition. You may want to check out Chella Quint's TEDx Talk 'Adventures in Menstruating' – it's very eye opening about menstrual taboos from history! (bit.ly/periodpositive)

Mostly Cs: The Period Denier

You're mortified by your periods and wish they never happened. But it's not your fault – and there's stuff you can do! Maybe the way you learned about them was tough going, or too little, too late. Or maybe you had to figure it out for yourself. Adverts don't help, that's for sure. You've never found the right language to discuss them, and often feel stifled and ashamed when thinking about them. It could be worthwhile exploring why you feel like this and try to find someone you can confide in when it comes to your monthly cycle. Talking about menstruation turns the subject from taboo to normal. Remember: there are currently around 334 million people on their periods as you are reading this. We need to find a way to talk through our period worries and personal experiences with one another. Check out www.periodpositive.com for a crash course in shame-free menstruation.

Period activism is a proactive movement to expose and combat the fact that periods are still very much stigmatized all over the world. There are now many 'movements' discussing menstruation frankly and openly online and beyond – from performance artists making statements in bloodied pants, to those shining a light on the lack of menstrual hygiene management in some poorer parts of the world.

Good hashtags to search on Twitter and Instagram for this are #PeriodChat and #PeriodPositive.

#PERIOD POSITIVE

#PERIOD CHAT

149

This section has been put together by the brilliant Chella Quint, comedian, menstruation education researcher and founder of #periodpositive. She presented an awesome TEDx Talk: Adventures in Menstruating: Don't Use Shame to Sell. (link again – bit.ly/periodpositive)

So there are four types of menstrual products. For real! You were probably thinking there were just two – pads and tampons, right? Most people – even parents and teachers, and definitely advertisers – tend to mention just these two! But there are four! Here's how I like to break it down . . .

Menstrual products can be:

Internal – worn inside your vagina.
External – worn inside your underwear, but outside your vagina.
Disposable – bought, worn once and then thrown away.
Reusable – bought, worn once, washed, dried and used again and again – for years!

Now – if you're seeing that reusable one and freaking out, you're not alone – but don't panic. We wash and reuse things that get stuff from our bodies on them all the time. We wash kitchen cutlery, mugs and glasses – and those get our spit on them. We wash our underwear and bed sheets too! . . . Unless you only wear disposable underwear, and your bed sheets come in a giant paper-towel roll, which you bin every morning, that is?!

So now that's cleared up, here are the four types again, along with the pros and cons of each one.

Internal (tampons, menstrual cups): You wear them inside your body so you can go swimming and – if you are a fashion maven – wear tight clothes without VMPL (visible menstrual product line!). On the negative side, some people don't like inserting tampons or menstrual cups into their vaginas – either they find it uncomfortable

MOON CUPS

generally, or they just haven't got the hang of it yet.

TAMPONS

External (disposable pads and cloth pads): These are great for when you first start menstruating, and some people swear by them for their whole lives. They can be more comfortable to wear when sleeping, and are easier to change without getting blood on your fingers. Some people find that pads feel really uncomfortable, a bit like a full nappy, when they get full of blood, though. And like our friend above, who learned the hard way . . . you definitely can't wear them swimming.

Disposable (disposable pads and tampons): They are convenient to get from a friend or quickly nip to the shop and buy if your period shows up a day early and you don't have a menstrual cup or cloth pad on you. They are expensive – some big-brand companies make huge profits, and use those profits to make loads of adverts . . . to sell more pads and tampons. It's a massive industry.

Reusable (cloth pads and menstrual cups): Good for the environment and for your wallet! One pad costs about the same as a box of disposable pads, but you can wash it, dry it and keep it for years. Menstrual cups come in different sizes to suit different body types and vagina shapes – and most companies have good return policies if they don't work for you. Cloth pads come in the same shapes, lengths and styles as disposable pads, but in way cuter patterns! You can't throw them away – so if you change it when you're out, you need to carry the used one in your handbag (in a ziplock bag or a small Tupperware box, or similar) until you get home and can put it in the wash.

Since all four types have different pros and cons, you might prefer to use a combination – maybe cloth pads at home at night; your menstrual cup during the day and on holiday; tampons in a pinch, when you realize you don't have your usual supplies with you; and disposable pads or pantyliners if your period means you're sensitive down there, or just don't feel like using something internally that day!

143

SANITARY TOWELS

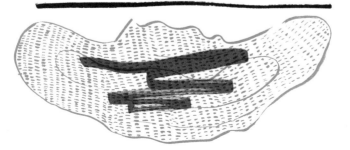

TOXIC SHOCK SYNDROME

What is it?

Toxic Shock Syndrome is a very rare but potentially life-threatening condition. It is caused by specific bacteria invading and releasing toxins into the blood-stream. TSS cases can occur in women, men and children. TSS can tend occur from localised infections like skin infections or in women who are having their periods and using tampons. TSS, although rare, is a medical emergency and it is important to have the knowledge about the symptoms and signs so you can seek early diagnosis and treatment.

Once TSS is diagnosed, emergency treatment of the bacterial infection with antibiotics and supportive treatment will be given in hospital to help your body cope with the toxins.

If you do use tampons, then it is really important to be aware of TSS and to be vigilant if you develop any symptoms of TSS and seek help immediately.

In general, if you are using tampons and suddenly get a high fever, aches, a rash, or flu-like symptoms, see your doctor immediately, because, while it's rare, TSS can go from looking like a simple illness to a really serious medical emergency very quickly, and you are way better safe than sorry!

Here are the symptoms:

Sudden high temperature
Flu-like symptoms – headache, cough, sore throat, muscle aches
Vomiting and/or nausea
Dizziness, fainting or feeling faint
Diarrhoea
A rash – a bit like sunburn
Confusion

If you develop any of these symptoms, you should contact a medical professional straight away to get their advice.

Advice from Dr Radha - my co-host on the Radio 1 *Surgery*, and all-round, energy-bringing beam of love - on what you should do if you think you've left a tampon in for too long

Change your tampon every four to six hours and never leave a tampon in for more than eight hours.

The best thing to do is to remove it as soon as you can if you think it has been in for too long.

You can normally feel the string or tampon to remove it yourself on most occasions. Sometimes it helps to put one leg up on a toilet seat and breathe in and out to relax when you are trying to find it.

Sometimes you cannot find the string or it is difficult to feel the tampon as it can move further up your vagina. If this is the case, then contact your GP straight away or the NHS helpline 111. They will endeavour to remove it immediately. If it is out of hours, then call the Out Of Hours GP helpline in your area or call 111, or attend A&E for help to remove the tampon straight away.

Tampon Tips

• Consider setting an alarm on your phone to remind you to remove your tampon.

• Never use more than one tampon at a time.

• Always wash your hands before changing your tampon and after.

• Always try to use the lowest absorbency for your period flow.

• Get to know your tampon brand and read the leaflet inside the pack.

• It is useful to think about alternating between tampons and pads while you have your period.

• Before you go to sleep while being on your period always think about putting in a fresh tampon and removing it as soon as you wake up.

If you are a trans or non-binary menstruator, this bit is for you

Not everyone who menstruates is a girl. And not all girls menstruate. If you're a trans guy or non-binary and you own a uterus, you have probably menstruated, or still do. You may not feel you fit into most conversations around menstruation, but there are loads of other trans and non-binary menstruators out there, and the conversation is (we agree, very slowly) changing. If you are out at school or college, and want to ensure you get support, ask friends, teachers and work colleagues of all genders to help you with the following:

* Use the word 'menstruator' to include everyone who menstruates.

* Try the phrases 'growing up' or 'going through puberty' or 'getting your first period' rather than saying someone is 'becoming a woman' to mean 'menstruating for the first time'.

* You might also consider asking that they re-label some toilets as unisex in your school, gig venue or workplace. If that's not possible right now, they should ensure there's a bin in cubicles in the gents' toilets as well, and that emergency menstrual products are available in there too.

BODY HAIR

OH, body hair. The epidemic of angst towards our own body hair drives me absolutely bananas. I have personally spent years of calamitously razor-rashing my poor downstairs, or going to waxing salons so they can painfully strip it off. SO horrendously embarrassing, I actually shudder at the thought of some of those trips over the years. I take my hat off to anyone who's completely comfortable with getting out their most private and intimate body parts for someone to tweeze, pour hot wax over, and yank hair out of with strips, whilst intensely crap, twinkly music pours out of speakers in an attempt to soothe those being plucked.

Our attitude towards female body hair is slightly twisted, really. When did it become 'attractive' to be so hairless? Free-and-easy access to porn has only exacerbated this obsession. NO ONE should tell us what we should do with our pubes. If you have a partner that does this, stick your tongue out and blow a firm raspberry in their face.

This goes for all hair, everywhere: under your armpits, coming out of your nostrils, on your arms and legs, on your upper lip, out of your bum, on your toes and around your belly button. Let it be your choice what you do or don't do with your hair – NEVER feel like you HAVE to do anything. Cos quite frankly you DON'T.

SPOTS

148

When I made a documentary about acne a few years ago for BBC3, I found myself flooded with emotional memories of the sadness and shame around having spotty skin, especially as a teenager.

I interviewed a young man who had not only had his confidence knocked by his severe acne, but had found it actually physically painful too, especially at night when he was lying on his bed, because he had acne on his back that was incredibly sore. He found it hard to look people in the eye and stooped his head low. He was prepared to do anything to get rid of it, though he had decided against taking what's often the 'last resort' prescribed by doctors and dermatologists – a drug called 'Roaccutane', which is linked to quite a lot of side-effects, from tiredness, to dry lips and even suicidal thoughts. He and his mum saved up for a year to have some private treatment involving light therapy, which in the end worked really well. BUT it wasn't cheap.

I learned a lot from making this doc – the biggest lessons being that there are many, many routes to clear skin. You just have to keep an open mind and not give up, make sure you research whatever you are prescribed (always) and that you read all the information that comes with prescribed drugs. Make decisions for yourself, and try not to get too bogged down. You also have to remember that acne is a universal issue, and that people don't judge you for having spots.

Another key thing to remember – very often, spots and acne are at their worst during the teenage years, and sometimes into your early twenties, but most people eventually grow out of it. Be patient. Keep calm. Things can only get better.

BODY IMAGE

> **❝** Every inch of our body, every aspect of our bodies, has been commercialized, either by the beauty companies, the cosmetic-surgery companies, the fashion houses, the food companies, the diet companies. So I think the situation's much worse, that our bodies are much more unstable . . . The situation with our bodies is pretty serious. We're sort of supposed to have our body as our product rather than the place we live from, and that's a really damaging concept. **❞**

Susie Orbach, author of seminal work *Fat is a Feminist Issue*. Her thoughts on women's relationships with their bodies these days are pretty clear.

We are bombarded with an overwhelming amount of images of unattainable bodies every minute of every day. According to recent stats, we check our phones up to 200 times a day on average. If most of that time is spent looking at the ideals we can never live up to, it's gonna be tough for our self-esteem to stay intact.

Body shaming is a complex issue. I'm fully aware that there is an argument for all body shapes, and that not one particular industry is to blame, especially with the swell of online activity adding petrol to the flames. Fitness trends and eating fads that are completely unregulated are reaching insane levels of popularity. How are we honestly supposed to find a balance when it comes to food, exercise and what our bodies should look like when we are bombarded with 'thinspiration', #bodygoals and the perfect thigh gap?

The truth is that some body shapes cannot be achieved unless a person dedicates their entire life to achieving it, monitoring everything that goes into it and denying themselves some of life's most wondrous things – like different types of food – and sacrificing for exercise time. So STOP. Listen to your body. Figure out what makes you feel healthy and wonderful – what food you find delicious and makes you feel happy inside. Find your own way of making your body bend, stretch, flex and work up a sweat (refer to EXERCISE on page 170 for more on this). It's your choice, and nobody else's.

What needs to be celebrated in society, and adored by ourselves and the mainstream media alike, is the HEALTHY body size – which is the body size we are each naturally supposed to be, and is different for all of us.

Take ownership and responsibility for yourself and for the 'brain food' you consume. Be careful about who you follow on Instagram, and check in with yourself to work out how what you're seeing is making you feel. Does it feel good to want a body shape that is difficult to attain . . . or is it hard work, miserable and counter-productive?

Do you find yourself agreeing with any of the following statements?

I wish I didn't look this way.

I often look at pictures of women's bodies in the media, and it makes me feel bad about my own body.

I find myself constantly researching and thinking of ways to try to look different to how I do now.

If you found yourself answering YES to any of the above, then it is time to actively work on your self-esteem and change some unhealthy online viewing habits.

I once interviewed two girls who told me that together they could spend up to six hours searching the word 'skinny' on Tumblr. It was only when they said that out loud that they realized that it wasn't doing them any good.

Start focusing on the bits of yourself that you do like, the bits that make you feel happy, strong and in control. People talk about eyes being beautiful because they are: go look at yours. They are your two portals to your inner galaxies: full of mermaid-tail blues, greys and greens, all the autumnal magic of brown, hazel and amber. Your eyes are breathtakingly beautiful.

The relentless and futile pursuit of perfection is all around us, and we have to find some way to cope with it, to see our bodies as not just good enough, but COOL AS F*CK! YOUR BODY IS VALUABLE AND REMARKABLE. The minute you accept that no one fits into the 'cookie cutter' of perfect, is the minute you will realize that all bodies are beautiful, including yours.

Personally, I want to live a life of extraordinary adventure, soul-igniting fun times, inquisitiveness and individuality . . . but I want to do it with my healthy, strong, NORMAL body.

As an experiment, I challenged my friends to draw their interpretation of their naked bodies on to an array of nude-(ish – it was way more difficult than I thought to buy the right skin-toned material!)-coloured body suits. I expected people to draw their self-portrait naturalistically, like I did – and I got on with colouring-in and thinking about what I look like with no clothes on. When I turned round, I realized everyone had gone rogue, and alternative body portraits were being created instead.

I loved the symbolism of this: the fact that our bodies can be WHATEVER WE WANT THEM TO BE.

153

Anna Hart: Swirly whirligig boobs and matching bush.

My body is mine, for feeling, using and enjoying. My body does not exist for other people to look at. Do something with your body that makes you feel strong and capable and free. Don't treat your body like an ornament.

Brigitte Aphrodite: Black lacy cycling shorts, and leaves on her boobs.

Your body is just a load of cells. When you look in the mirror, don't obsess over the finer details — do a wiggle, just to see if you like the way your clothes swing, check for bogeys and then go.

Jessica Jordan-Wrench: All-seeing, all-knowing eyes for boobs.

Long walks, short swims and exuberant dancing outshines calorie counting. In so many ways.

Me: Chocolate-button-brown nips, and a big proud bush.

My body usually responds well to its environment. If I am in the gym, it will suddenly, when pushed, be quite strong; my feet didn't ache too much when I trekked up Mount Kenya; and it responds brilliantly to a cuddle.

Emma Gibson: Smiley face for pregnant tummy.

No one really cares what you look like; they are too busy thinking about how they look themselves.

Zezi Ifore: Bowie-inspired lightning-bolt body contouring.

Dress sizes in shops are totally meaningless. Try stuff on (ESPECIALLY if buying vintage!), and if you feel mega/cool as hell/fabulous, then get it. Anything less, leave it behind. Greater treasures await!

Frances Acquaah:
#BlackLivesMatter tattoo,
pom-pom, bunny-tail bum.

*Images of perfection are
shoved in our faces at
every possible opportunity,
and I am more self-
conscious than I have ever
been. Everything will
change very quickly. In
all things, embrace the
present. You will blink and
it will be ten years later!*

Laura Cairney-Keize:
Purple-star vagina.

*Your body changes
constantly — if you
look after it, it will
look after you.*

**Georgia Lewis-
Anderson:** Psychedelic
purple daisies for
boobs.

*Dress sizes in shops
can be confusing and
totally vary. I'm
actually a different
size on the top and
bottom.*

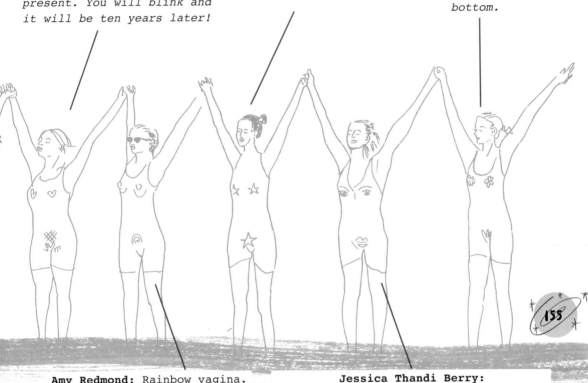

155

Amy Redmond: Rainbow vagina.

*I wish I had known when I
was a teenager that true
happiness comes from within;
that staring in the mirror
won't change anything;
and that wasting your
time, energy and thoughts
on ways to look thinner is
exactly that, a waste.*

Jessica Thandi Berry:
Lips on lips.

*The most extraordinary part of my body
isn't a physical thing. I have pretty
vivid and crazy dreams, so the part
of the brain that can dream is pretty
extraordinary to me.*

SHOW US YOUR BODY STORY

Use the colour code below to show your story.

● has seen me through adventure

● is gentle

● has overcome something

● is strong

● I love this part

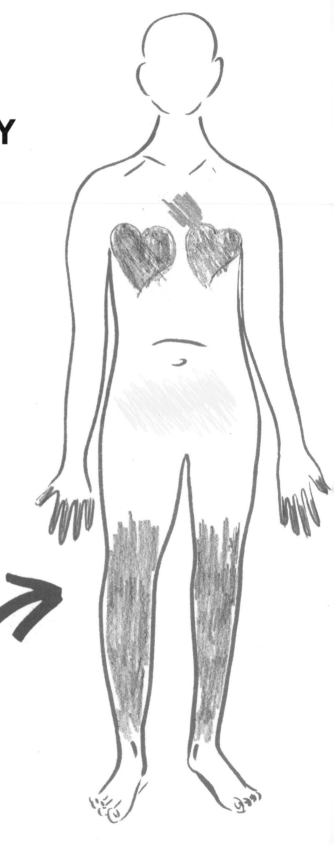

this is mine

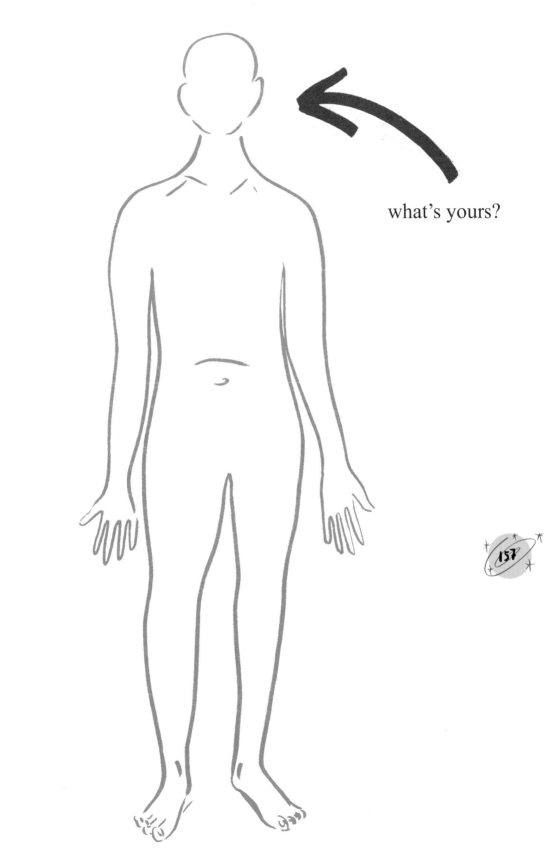

what's yours?

157

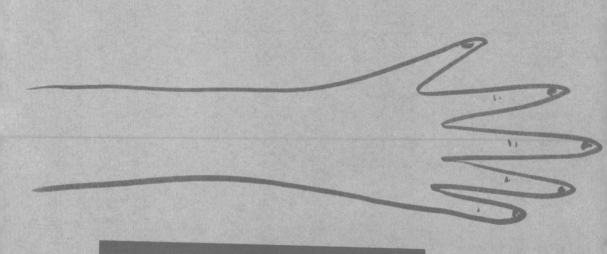

SPANDANGLE THE BITS YOU LOVE

If you like certain parts of your body, then show them off that bit more. It can be any bit: your wrists (get the sparkliest watch); your nose (get a buzz-cut and show off your nose proudly to the world); your calves (roll up your jeans and wear rainbow-coloured socks pulled up); your bum bum (shake it, shake it); your tum tum – no matter the size! Don't be afraid of sunnier climes and the notion of whether you're 'bikini body ready'. Personally, I love a swimming costume – for me, they are (and always will be) so much more fun to wear than a bikini. They stay on when you jump in the water; they protect you more from the sun. Don't get me started on the reasons I love a swimming costume! Well, if you insist . . .

158

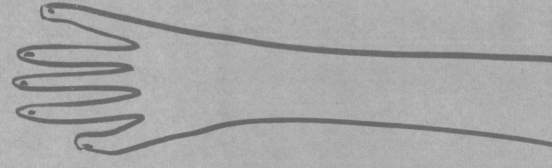

Reasons I love a swimming costume (the mini manifesto):

* They make me feel 'held in'. Feeling 'held in' is good. It makes you feel more bendy – and less self-conscious when you want to cartwheel on the beach.

* The leg of a cossie is often more 'realistically' cut for bushes. Yep – PUBIC HAIR AGAIN.

* If you buy a vintage one (do, and give it a boil wash) or one designed like a vintage one (which you can very easily online), you can ACTUALLY feel like a Hollywood star from the 1950s.

* If you look hard enough, you can even get a 'SWIM DRESS' – an actual dress to swim in! One step beyond a swimming costume, it's like a full dress, and in my opinion is the dream – covering your nether regions, swaying with sass as you sashay around the pool.

Having said all that, if you want to wear a bikini and your stomach is not like a washboard, then you're going to look beautiful too. Don't hide your loveliness if you don't want to. Whatever makes you feel good, and comfortable – you do YOU.

159

COLOUR ME IN!

CLOTHES

They can give your soul the most fabulous lift.

I love clothes. My eyes are always on stalks for fabric that is bold and that glistens, for opportunities to experiment with colours and patterns that bring bursts of joy, ridiculousness and fun to my soul and stir my imagination. My clothes represent all the things that I'm made of, all the different things that I feel. I like to shop for clothes when I'm in far-flung places, on holidays and trips, so that I have mementos of times when at my happiest that I can wrap around me to keep me warm. I honestly get lost in my own faraway land of contentment when I look at old tank tops, Tropicana-printed pyjama-type trousers and denim (that looks like it's been worn by someone who's rolled around for hours on a chalky moon) in vintage shops. I sometimes wish I could actually eat the shoes they make me so happy – they are like sweets, delicious-looking, big shiny 1970s ones that scream and shout disco and dazzling, platform-defying dance moves.

The only real fashion advice I will give in this book is to flip OPEN the lid on your creativity. Never be frightened to wear whatever and be whoever you want to be. Experience the joy of showing off your identity through clothes. If for you that means following a tribe, a cultural scene, or opting to express yourself through clothes of certain cultural significance . . . then that's cool. If it means wearing all the shades of black and grey, then that's cool too. If it's wanting to wear a ball gown to a BBQ, then do it. The most sublimely dressed are those who look like they love what they are wearing.

Dressing SEXY

Sexiness is great if that's a look you choose to inhabit. But only if you are happy dressing that way. Ask yourself at least three times before you go out if you are comfortable in what you are wearing. The secret to sexiness is that it doesn't come from showing lots of skin, or wearing a specific outfit or piece of clothing – it comes from CONFIDENCE. Sexiness can be found and achieved in the loosest of loose kaftans that swirls around your body, or a pair of dungarees that makes you skip down the street. Your happiness, your delight, your ease with what you're wearing will be infectious.

And that is sexy.

A Warning on short Shorrrrrrttttttsssssss...

By Gem

Beware of the teeny weeny, tiny whiny, squeeeeeny little denim shorts,
cos if your front crack could talk
it would go on rants,
it prefers longer pants.
Shorts go up your bum,
make festivals less fun,
hours of camel toe,
the worst fanny foe.
Legs sticking to seats,
no protection from heat,
leave the peach exposers
to the fashion posers.
Just beware of the teeny weeny, tiny whiny little denim shorts.

163

Isn't it ironic?

Everyone wants what they don't have, right? Those with gloriously curly hair will spend hours upon hours straightening it. Those with brown hair will dye it bright red, and vice versa. Those with small busts want massive bajongas; but those with massive bajongas long for a smaller bust. Shorties look at tall types with green-eyed envy; but then tall types feel self-conscious and wish to be shorter.

Upon research into the 'ideal body', I heard the following statements:

You've gotta have big boobs.

You've gotta have a big bum.

You've gotta have a tiny waist.

You've gotta have a thigh gap.

When you see these things all together, it's a bit ironic, right? A contradiction. Each body description jumps from one to another, and an overwhelming desire for them all could be damaging. I hardly have to spell this out – as most of us know from our own bodies, or those of our mums, sisters and friends – but women with big bums don't often have tiny waists; women with tiny waists don't often have big boobs; and so on. (I know of course there are exceptions, but let's generalize for a moment.)

Without name-checking certain figures of prominence in popular culture, I'm keen to make one thing clear – those that do somehow have all these features together, those that embody all these 'ideals', have usually gone beyond normal lengths to achieve their body shape: exercising an excessive amount, having teams of people that airbrush or enhance and manipulate the images they put out there of themselves. Some of them have even spent lots of money on surgery. People don't naturally have the shape of Jessica Rabbit – Jessica Rabbit is a cartoon character (google her if you don't know who she is).

Psssst – I do love a fabulous cartoon character! Rastamouse, for example, has impeccable dress sense, and Little My from the Moomins is a badass. Plus, when I'm in a mood, some say I have a likeness to Sarah the Dinosaur in *A Land Before Time* . . . (honestly, google and watch them all immediately if you're not familiar with any of these characters). But I'm fully aware they are not real people; they are just cartoons.

PERFECT

THE ONLY
MAKE-UP TIP
>>> if you like make-up,
use it as your war paint
rather than your 'flaw-
covering' paint.

What is 'perfect'?

Perfect [*adjective*]
Having all the required or desirable elements, qualities,
or characteristics; as good as it is possible to be.

Examples:
'She strove to be the **perfect** wife.'
'Life certainly isn't **perfect** at the moment.'

Interesting that striving to be the 'perfect' wife
and wanting a 'perfect' life are used as examples.

WELL, YOU KNOW WHAT...
I'M SICK OF PERFECT!

I will never be anybody's perfect anything. What a waste of time to strive to be a 'perfect wife'. I would rather 'strive' to have a fun night out, 'strive' for an endorphin rush from swimming in open waters, 'strive' to travel to as many places on the earth as I can and holiday with all my friends, 'strive' to have a house filled with fun and lovely things to look at, especially sunflowers. But, even if I achieved all those things, my life still wouldn't be 'perfect' – because there's no such thing. In fact, I think the only thing that can be considered 'perfect' is a delicious doughnut, just when you are craving a doughnut more than anything.

PROTECT YOUR SOUL FROM
THE FEAR OF IMPERFECTION

Sorry to sound harsh, but I can tell you now it's POINTLESS to fear imperfection. That I can promise you. We are big knotty tangles of ups and downs, triumphs and landslides. It's what makes us human.

No lipstick-painted smile can hide it. No tiny waist, wedding ring, lottery win or grade-A exam result can make someone wholly perfect. The trouble is that we now have the technology and the mindset to make ourselves appear perfect – and, in doing so, we just reinforce the idea that this false sense of 'perfection' is desirable and attainable. Things like bodies, jobs, weddings and other big life situations – they can all look perfect on a screen where they can be so easily exaggerated and filtered and edited. (Think about the last time you used a filter to turn a quite boring social activity into what looked like the most fun thing EVER!) But, more than that, you can actually manipulate your face and body using apps to give yourself the smoothest skin, the boobs you want, legs just a bit longer, eyes just a bit bigger. Read that back. Does it frighten you as much as it frightens me?

#RelationshipGoals   #BodyGoals   #SquadGoals   #HashtagEverything!

This is what I sometimes read as an alternative caption when I look at selfies on social media:

The truth is I haven't eaten breakfast today and I feel tired.

The truth is I worry about my looks all the time.

The truth is, looking back at my last ten Insta pictures, I was having a bad day during at least four of those pics, and I don't really like who I've got my arm round in three.

The truth is I've spent many hours of my life working out how to take the best picture.

The truth is I get lonely.

Nobody's actually perfect. Next time you're feeling shitty when you're comparing yourself to other people, unfollow or unfriend those accounts or profiles that make you feel that way. It's time to work out and break down what is feeding this inner yearning to be PERFECT, and to protect ourselves from the negative influence and sense of misery it leaves us with.

VANITY CULTURE

So, from every angle we are subjected to a huge amount of pressure to embody what society says is beautiful – earlier pages have established that. The harsh reality is that in some extreme cases girls as young as fourteen are having cosmetic procedures to make their faces more 'beautiful'. It comes back to what we're seeing on social media and TV and the rapidly obsessive selfie culture isn't helping.

These days, we are ALWAYS looking at ourselves. Think about our parents. Back when they were teens, they probs only caught their reflection a few times a day: in the morning when they were brushing their teeth, a few times during the day when heading to the loo and then last thing at night when they brushed their teeth again! Now think of all the pictures you've ever seen of them when they were your age. Think about the grainy warmth of printed film photography, its calmness. Think of their faces in the pictures, not overly self-conscious, just smiling, in the moment – NOT worried about what that picture is going to look like straight away a few minutes before they put it online or send it to a friend. They knew that they had to wait until it was printed to see it. Living in the moment, oblivious and carefree, equals natural beauty. Yes, I have personally taken selfies, of course, but I try not to pay too much mind to the way I look. It's something I've almost trained myself to do – to not scrutinize myself too much, and to try to live in the moment.

I've said it before: some insecurity about how you look is part of life, especially as we are constantly changing – it can be hard to keep up sometimes; it can be awkward. The bad news is that so-called 'solutions' such as fillers, Botox or cosmetic surgery are more readily available and more affordable than ever, and sometimes conducted by less-than-qualified people. It is now considered acceptable for some young people to pay for these procedures. If you are considering having or have become preoccupied with the idea of cosmetic surgery – please think deep in your soul whether it's something you need to be happy.

I once interviewed two cosmetic surgeons for a show I covered on the BBC World Service called *The Conversation*. Nothing was going to stop me from finding out as much as possible from two women who put people under the knife for their jobs – I was fascinated by them. One doctor was working in Colombia, South America, and practised cosmetic surgery, paid for by people who wanted to change something they didn't like about themselves. And the other doctor was working in South Korea, and mainly operated on those who were in need, reconfiguring those born with a deformity or who'd been disfigured by an accident or disease.

Both surgeons talked about the trends in cosmetic surgery in their parts of the world. In South Korea, women of all ages want more 'Western-shaped' eyes – that is, for their eyes to be made more round than the traditional almond shape. In Colombia, many women want smaller waists and bigger boobs and bums, like Jessica Rabbit (who I mentioned earlier).

The more the surgeons spoke, the more exasperated and sick I felt. I learned that in Colombia women as young as fourteen sometimes have 'surgery' birthday parties, where they would get a new nose. I heard tales of women coming to consultations convinced that their lives would be so much better if only they didn't look the way they did. And I found out how it felt for both surgeons to be asked to operate on their friends and family. Self-hate is a global issue, I thought. How have we got to a place where at the age of fourteen we are prepared to have our bones cracked to reform them, or have fat sucked from our stomachs and thighs just to, supposedly, look better in clothes?

My aim isn't to shame an entire industry, and there is nothing wrong with taking your own kind of pride in how you look, in feeling your type of best. All I know is that I want to beg young women to rid themselves of the maddening insecurity that is at a saddening all-time high, all over the world. All I can keep doing is telling you, reader, that you are so beautiful, I promise you. Beautiful, just the way you are. I am on my knees, begging you to remember this fact. Even if in the past you felt one way, and now you feel another. You were and always will be BEAUTIFUL.

EXERCISE

First of all, exercise is good for us. It just is. It helps to keep our bodies
healthy and it protects us from disease. We need to move our butts.
That said, exercise can be taken to extremes and become an addiction
(see pages 93–4) and it is important to keep perspective on it. Some people are
naturally athletic and sporty; some people are more inclined to take it easier. Whatever
type you are, go with your natural rhythm, get your heart beating, your blood circulating,
but don't obsess about it. That is counter-productive.

My philosophy: move ya body in a way that feels right to you rather than in a way
dictated by someone else. We should not be in competition with our friends when it comes to
exercise – we know what's right for us; we take our own breaths.

I love to move, whether it is to bend in satisfying lunges, roll my head around in circular
motions on the end of my neck like a Jabberwock, or to shake ma tail feather like a Queen
Bee doing the 'Waggle' dance. To move is one of the magic things about having a body: it
aligns and centres us and creates a kind of euphoria that I adore. I'm all for the endorphins
that exercise release – for feeling good in our minds and in our limbs, for feeling happy and
strong. But a great body is not one that has been pushed and pummelled and exhausted on a
daily basis. A great body is one that zings with health and energy.

The best exercise is that which benefits our minds and our bodies. Our inner fitness motor
engine will work better if it is fuelled by a love of taking part in an activity, rather than feeling
a pressure to push ourselves unnaturally far and turning what should be fun into obsessional
behaviour.

Stop counting, start dancing. Constant clocking of calories-to-cardio ratio is a waste of
time and, quite frankly, A BORE. It even bores *you*, admit it.

I asked founder of the Equus gym, body-positive, fitness-balancing delight and personal
trainer **Nic Addison** her thoughts on reaching a healthy attitude towards exercise:

> It really is simple: my job as a personal trainer is to get more
> people, more active, more often.
>
> It is important to recognize that activity and movement does
> not mean hitting the gym four times a week! Any movement will be
> of benefit to your mind, body and spirit.
>
> It's easy to get confused, overwhelmed and intimidated by
> hard-hitting media on the subject. HIT (high intensity) workouts,
> strength training, charcoal smoothies . . .

LET'S START WITH MOVEMENT

For health benefits – not even fitness or fat loss – we <u>MUST</u> walk for thirty minutes every single day. That's not four times a week, that's not power walking up Everest, it's simply walking at your pace for thirty minutes every single day. Sounds easy? Pop a decent pair of shoes on and start TODAY!

THEN THERE IS THE 80/20 RULE

Adopt a mindful approach to your food, exercise, sleep, stress choices for eighty per cent of the time and allow for flexibility for the remaining twenty per cent. The 80/20 rule is all about setting realistic goals – accepting that we cannot be perfect, and patting ourselves on the back when we achieve that eighty per cent. Achieving eighty per cent across the board will see rapid, consistent, sustainable body results. I am forever telling my clients that being consistently good at eighty per cent is far better than being inconsistently excellent at a hundred per cent!

80 / 20%

PERMISSION

Following the 80/20 rule gives you complete power and the permission to enjoy your life.

The 80/20 rule for me means that for five days of the week I won't have that biscuit with my mid-morning cuppa; I will opt for a sparkling water over the bottle of BrewDog in the fridge; I will ensure protein is in every meal; I will make sure I go to bed at a decent time. For two days of the week I enjoy my curry, have that drink, go to bed a bit later, eat some Maltesers and just basically live guilt-free with a smug smile on my face.

MOVEMENT FOR RESULTS

ON TOP of our daily thirty minutes of walking for health, when you are seeking results relating to achieving your fitness goals, that's when 'exercise' comes in to play. Exercise that makes your heart pump, your forehead sweaty and your fingers and toes tingly three times a week for a minimum of twenty minutes will see you achieve those results.

Initially it doesn't matter what the mode of exercise is. It's the adherence that is key. So, if you like Zumba, do Zumba. If football is your thing – do that. If you love making loud exercise noises in your lounge to a fitness DVD, do that three times a week, consistently, for a few weeks.

So, chase endorphins by bowling about the park with your mates. Move, stretch, go dancing. BREATHE. Don't get trapped in a spider's web of feeling like you have to try to achieve something just because you've seen it on Instagram. Yes, go to the gym, if that's your thing, but exercise should not have to cost loads of money. If you're going to get a personal trainer, do some research. It's cheaper to share one, for instance. Try something before committing to it. Check your compatibility with it. Not everything is for everyone.

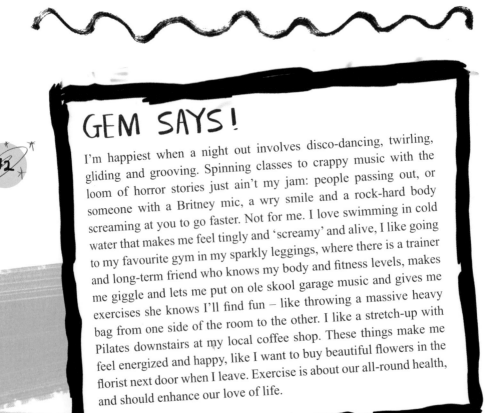

GEM SAYS!

I'm happiest when a night out involves disco-dancing, twirling, gliding and grooving. Spinning classes to crappy music with the loom of horror stories just ain't my jam: people passing out, or someone with a Britney mic, a wry smile and a rock-hard body screaming at you to go faster. Not for me. I love swimming in cold water that makes me feel tingly and 'screamy' and alive, I like going to my favourite gym in my sparkly leggings, where there is a trainer and long-term friend who knows my body and fitness levels, makes me giggle and lets me put on ole skool garage music and gives me exercises she knows I'll find fun – like throwing a massive heavy bag from one side of the room to the other. I like a stretch-up with Pilates downstairs at my local coffee shop. These things make me feel energized and happy, like I want to buy beautiful flowers in the florist next door when I leave. Exercise is about our all-round health, and should enhance our love of life.

Fun ways to get sweaty, provided by Nic:

QUICK EVERYDAY ACTIVITY TIPS

1. Get active every day!

You can burn 250kcal more each day increasing incidental movements – walk when on the phone, do housework, even fidgeting will make a difference. Remember, exercise is not expensive and can actually save money! Simple things like washing the car or vacuuming the carpet will get the heart pumping and the muscles working.

2. Learn and love the squat!

Every workout should include some kind of squatting movement. A squat is the staple of all great exercise programmes. Bottom line is that making improvements to the way you look and feel starts with the squat.

3. Get crawling!

Crawling is massively underrated and is not just for babies! Crawling refines both gross and fine motor skills by strengthening the large and small muscle groups. It is also fantastic for brain stimulation and creating a spike in the heart rate.

4. Hit the dance floor!

Dancing can burn 400 calories per hour! So pop on your favourite song and dance around your living room.

DYNAMIC STRETCH WORKOUT

It's not always about lifting heavy weights or having the best ever workout, beating your personal best! Sometimes we just need to move. Sometimes we just need to breathe and relax. Sometimes we just need to get the blood pumping. This is the workout that will do just that and will take around twenty minutes. The exercises below are suitable for everyone, of any age or fitness ability. No equipment is needed.

1.

To start off. Complete each move in order only once. Move as quickly or as slowly as you like. This workout is about range of movement rather than repetitions or pace, so take your time and exaggerate every move.

- March on the spot for twenty steps.
- Complete ten shoulder circles: hands touching the shoulders; complete big circles of the elbows.
- Complete ten torso twists: hands touching the elbows; take a wide stance and twist the torso.
- Complete ten knee hugs: raise one knee at a time and hug it into your chest; alternate legs, five on each side.
- Complete ten heel kicks: bring one heel to the buttocks; alternate, ten each side.
- Complete ten toe touches: push a leg out to the side, reach forward and touch the toe. Repeat.

- Complete ten back taps: raise one arm high, bend at the elbow and touch between your shoulder blades with your hand. Alternate and complete ten on each side.

2.

Read on for a more technical, dynamic work-out. Complete three of each move then move on to the next exercise.

- Stand tall, breathe in and reach both hands as high as you can in the air, shrug the shoulders, lifting your chest and lift up on to your tiptoes.
- Place heels back on the floor, breathe out and bend forward at the hips, taking your hands forward and then down towards your toes, stretching your hamstrings. Take a breath and rise back to standing. Repeat.

- Stand, then crawl forward on to your hands and into a push-up position. Pause then crawl back up to standing. Repeat.
- Stand, then crawl back into a press-up position. Lower your hips to the floor, lift your chest and draw back the shoulders. Lower chest back to the floor. Repeat.
- Lying on the floor, bring your heels towards the buttocks, reach back to grip your feet at the laces and clench buttocks to stretch the front of the thigh. Release the legs back to the floor. Take a breath. Repeat.
- Push your body back up into a push-up position, walk the hands back, place palms on the thighs and push up to stand up.

3.

Now a little slower to finish . . .

- Complete five shoulder circles: hands touching the shoulders; complete big circles of the elbows.
- Complete five torso twists: hands touching the elbows, take a wide stance and twist the torso.
- Complete five knee hugs: raise one knee at a time and hug it into your chest; alternate legs, five on each side.
- Complete five toe touches: push a leg out to the side, reach forward and touch the toe. Repeat.
- Complete five back taps; raise one arm high, bend at the elbow and touch between your shoulder blades with your hand. Alternate and complete five on each side.

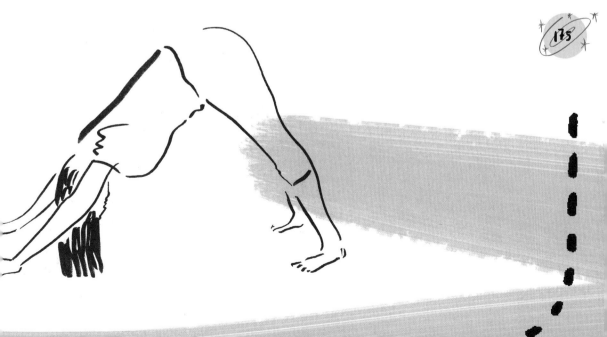

FOOD, GLORIOUS FOOOOD

Gobble, gobble, gobble. Someone at the top of the advertising food chain is making bucket-loads of cash. Gobble, gobble, gobble. You'd think that the mine of information we can access about what we should and shouldn't eat would make dietary experts out of us all these days. That we'd be sophisticated and highly informed, with superb food and nutrition knowledge.

Unfortunately it's a little more confusing than that, and there's almost too much information, much of it conflicting, and lots of non-qualified people out to make a quick buck by offering 'aspirational foodie lifestyles'. How healthy are these eating plans really? To get a view from a bona fide expert, I talked to Leo Pemberton, a registered dietitian and nutritionist, who works with people and organizations advising on healthy eating and diet. The full interview with Leo is available as an *OPEN* podcast. It's useful. Go listen to it!

There are a couple of trends that do worry me. One would be the clean-eating movement. At first glance, that doesn't appear to be dangerous . . . but it can lead to disordered eating, because if you start to cut out lots of different food groups . . . only go for raw foods instead of cooked foods, for example, or if you're going gluten free, then going vegan, on top of that, suddenly you're left with not very much in your diet, or maybe only vegetables or only one food group. It can spiral.

One of the dangerous things is that if you follow certain bloggers or Instagram stars, they will all have a slightly different ethos . . . It's not necessarily backed up by science; their advice may swing dramatically from what your goals are. Lots of people want to follow a healthy diet for weight loss, and there are lots of ways you can lose weight, but if you're cutting out vitamins and minerals and things like calcium or protein from your diet — especially if you're still growing or you're very active — that's when it becomes dangerous and you can run into deficiencies, for example.

There are some very good people out there who do give sound advice. But on the flipside a lot of personal trainers or fitness gurus will also claim to be nutrition or fitness experts, and the advice that they often give out is either wrong or misleading, or they have their own theories on what is good in terms of nutrition.

One of the issues I have with some food bloggers and personalities out there is sometimes they can be very, very slim, which isn't a problem — lots of people are naturally slimmer. But it's this image and how they portray it with Instagram or certain blogs that make people want to buy into the 'slimness' posed as nutrition. Whereas the reality is it might not be their diet or their lifestyle that has contributed to their look.

I think, in general, we have to be very careful when we start following or copying what someone else is doing.

In terms of the link between the trends and the clean-eating movement and anorexia, I don't think the link is incredibly clear yet. However, I'm certainly seeing a lot of people who appear to be suffering from the symptoms of what we've termed orthorexia — cutting out many food groups to the point where that has an effect on everyday life, and duties, and socializing for example. That's certainly something that I'm seeing.

The bottom line should be that you can be a healthy body weight, live a long life, have a healthy skeleton and live a successful life, having a balanced diet including all food groups in your diet.

"

WHAT IS ORTHOREXIA?

orthorexia [*noun*]

An obsession with eating foods that one considers healthy. A medical condition in which the sufferer systematically avoids specific foods that they believe to be harmful.

If you are feeling concerned or confused by your own eating habits, or someone else's, please head to the back of this book, where there is a list of organizations that will be able to offer you specific advice.

SEX

Let's talk about it. Sex, after all (whether we like it or not), is how we exist. Our bodies and souls are so connected to our relationship with sex and everything that surrounds it: who we love, who we fancy, how we choose to explore those feelings, and the decisions that we and those close to us make when it comes to sex and sexuality.

THE LEGAL BIT

The age of consent for any form of sexual activity is sixteen for both men and women. The age of consent is the same regardless of the gender or sexual orientation of a person and whether the sexual activity is between people of the same or different gender.

It is an offence for anyone to have any sexual activity with a person under the age of sixteen.

It is an offence for a person aged eighteen or over to have any sexual activity with a person under the age of eighteen if the older person holds a position of trust (for example, a teacher or social worker) as such sexual activity is an abuse of the position of trust.

If there was an aisle for 'sex' in the supermarket, it'd be somewhere between the golden syrup and the treacle – all tempting and gloopy. It drip, drips into our brains, confusing us, exciting us, making us giggle. It's a subject that at some point in our lives most of us will experience in some way. But if you are yet to experience it, it can be a daunting, scary, BIG thing.

Sex is personal. Not just because it is an intimate act, but because it is individual to each of us. We are each comfortable with different things, and we each have our own pace. When you're a teenager, it is easy to feel pressured into it – either by other people or by yourself. Sex seems to be all around us, online, on TV, on advertising billboards, on magazine covers. It's easy to feel that everyone is doing it, and doing it right.

But it is up to you, and only you, how you feel about sex. Not what your friends say, or what you may have watched online or in a film. YOU are the keeper of your body and soul, and when it comes to doing it, it needs to be a consensual, respectful act between you and your partner. Consensual sex is not just a physical act; it is an emotional one too. And it has consequences – ranging from feeling vulnerable and strange, to becoming pregnant or contracting an STD. Before you do it, prepare yourself, make sure you are safe. It's so important to explore what we are personally comfortable with and to think it through before we do it. It is ALWAYS one hundred per cent fine to say NO. It is ALWAYS OK to express yourself and say how you feel when it comes to sex. If you don't want to do it for any reason, then under no circumstances do you have to.

Your body is nobody's but yours. Be confident and sure about the person with whom you choose to share it. And always, always, ALWAYS make sure you are feeling safe and comfortable.

Me? I'm continuously confused by sex. My feelings towards sex change all the time. What it is, what it means to me, how much I like it, and what I like about it. It changes depending on who you're with, how you are feeling in your soul, what's going on in your life outside the partnership, how you are feeling about your health and your body at any given time. In essence, I think it's best to just accept that we'll never have all the answers, and just when we think we're crystal clear in our opinions, thoughts, wants and desires . . . they will change again. As long as we are being safe and considering each and every sexual decision we make, then we can control how vulnerable it makes us.

FIVE THINGS SEX SHOULD BE

1 Within your boundaries, which you have the right to change at any time, according to how you feel.

2 Mutually fun and caring.

3 FULLY CONSENSUAL for everyone involved.

4 With someone you trust and think is great.

5 SAFE.

FIVE THINGS SEX SHOULDN'T BE

1 Pressured or forced.

2 Uncomfortable or consistently painful.

3 Putting your sexual health at risk.

4 With someone you don't trust.

5 Shared online or with strangers against your wishes or without your knowledge.

SEXUALITY

Who we are and who we share our love and intimacy with is a decision more personal than nearly anything else in our lives. This doesn't make it any easier if you are feeling confused or you are worried about what people might think of your sexuality.

REMEMBER: do not feel you have to define your sexuality to anyone if you don't want to.

182

Personal trainer and presenter Georgie Okell opens up on her experience of coming out.

"The things we tell ourselves can be quite amazing. The stories we create in our own minds. The stories we allow to build and grow and extend so far into and across our consciousness that they begin to obscure what is real.

One of the stories I had created by my second year of university went like this: if everyone finds out you're gay, you're going to have to leave. Leave this uni, leave this town, start again. How embarrassing. How utterly inconvenient. Best to keep that information under wraps. Better to have cool friends and be popular and date boys you don't fancy just so you look the part. Better, even, to have a girlfriend you keep secret, who you meet up with late at night, whose calls you don't answer when you're with friends. Who you are utterly in love with but ashamed to be seen with, in case anyone figures out the terrible truth.

I'd known for ages, of course. I remember kissing a girl at fourteen and feeling the entire world melt around us, like nothing else existed. My brain was all fireworks and explosions; my heart practically bursting out of my chest. Despite that, I deemed those feelings undesirable. I decided maybe it might be best and sensible if I ignored them and definitely didn't talk about them. I hoped, actually, that they might go away and I'd never have to feel those wonderful feels about a girl ever again.

Thankfully, love and lust don't work like that. The fireworks kept coming back, refusing to be ignored into submission. So around the age of nineteen, I began to acknowledge them, begrudgingly. I certainly didn't accept them, though, nor did I think it wise to share how I felt with anyone lest people look at me differently. Heaven forbid. What other people thought about me was the single most important thing in the world and, as long as I continued to fit in, I'd be just fine.

My coming-out story is underwhelming. Get ready: one night at university in my second year, I was stood outside a house party with my two (straight) best friends, and they said, 'Georgie, we know you have a girlfriend. We don't care.' Just like that. That was the huge coming-out moment I had dreaded and

feared. Over in an instant. My internal relief and joy was much, much bigger than the moment itself, and I felt an overwhelming sense of everything shifting. In that one moment, I knew I was on the path to opening up and being myself. That path hasn't always been easy or comfortable. There have been bumps in the road, difficult periods with my family and their acknowledgment of my sexuality. Letters I wrote which were met with gaping silence from those not willing to hear what I was telling them. It has taken me the best part of a decade to be truly, truly comfortable with being an out-and-proud gay woman who can talk about it, write about it, shout about it from the rooftops.

I knew that for sure when I finally started to stand up for myself and not allow other people to decide how I was portrayed in the public sphere. I remember

184

particularly presenting a television show in the US a couple of years ago and being told to walk differently, talk differently, grow my hair, wear more make-up, talk about male pop stars in a way that might suggest I fancied them. I declined to do any of the above. I look how I look. I feel how I feel. I love who I love. Take it or leave it.

Being different certainly tests our sense of self, to step out of what is easy and acceptable and start to shape and define ourselves as an individual — it's scary. But taking ownership of all that makes us wholly and truly ourselves. It's the single most important thing we can do. To ignore or conceal any aspect of who we really, truly are, to live uncomfortably in a skin that doesn't quite fit instead of comfortably in our own is weirdly easy,

but it's also a waste. A waste of all the little things that make you you.

I'm lucky — the bumpy road I've stumbled along for the past decade is nothing compared to the mountains I know some have climbed just to be able to have their sexuality acknowledged. Honesty and openness require bravery, but if there is one thing in life worth fighting for it is the ability to be completely ourselves, and to love genuinely and wholeheartedly. Stories are great, but the truth is always greater.

185

GENDER AND SEXUALITY

It's important that we equip ourselves with the tools of communication when it comes to the distinct issues of gender, sexual orientation and sexuality. It is powerful and special to be able to talk about these things. It enables us to try to understand ourselves and those around us.

Glossary of terms and definitions for the realms of gender and sexuality

Provided by Suran Dickson, founder of Diversity Role Models (DRM). DRM tackles bullying related to gender and sexuality and encourages critical thinking by taking positive role models into schools.

A

Ally: a (typically) straight and/or cisgender person who supports members of the LGBTQ (lesbian, gay, bisexual, transsexual and queer) community .

B

Asexual: someone who does not experience sexual attraction

Biphobia: the fear or dislike of someone who identifies as bisexual.

Bisexual or bi: refers to a person who has an emotional and/or sexual orientation towards more than one gender.

C

Cisgender or cis: a person whose gender identity is the same as the sex they were assigned at birth. 'Non-trans' is also used by some people.

Coming out: when a person first tells someone/others about their identity.

D

Deadnaming: calling someone by their birth name after they have changed their name. This term is often associated with transsexual people who have changed their name as part of their transition.

G

Gay: refers to a man who has an emotional, romantic and/or sexual orientation towards men. Also a generic term for lesbian and gay sexuality – some women define themselves as gay rather than lesbian.

Gender dysphoria: when a person experiences discomfort or distress because there is a mismatch between their sex assigned at birth and their gender identity. This is also the clinical diagnosis for someone who doesn't feel comfortable with the gender they were born with.

Gender identity: a person's internal sense of their own gender, whether male, female or something else (see 'non-binary' below).

Gender queer: someone who doesn't identify with traditional binary gender roles, and instead identifies as neither, both, or a combination of them.

Gender reassignment: another way of describing a person's transition. To undergo gender reassignment usually means to undergo some sort of medical intervention, but it can also mean changing names, pronouns, dressing differently and living in their self-identified gender. Gender reassignment is protected by the Equality Act 2010.

Gender Recognition Certificate (GRC): this enables trans people to be legally recognized in their self-identified gender and to be issued with a new birth certificate. Not all trans people will apply for a GRC, and you have to be over eighteen to apply. You do not need a GRC to change your gender at work or to legally change your gender on other documents such as your passport.

Gender stereotypes: the ways that we expect people to behave in society according to their gender, or what is commonly accepted as 'normal' for someone of that gender.

Gender variant: someone who does not conform to the gender roles and behaviours assigned to them at birth. This is often used in relation to children or young people.

Heterosexual/straight: refers to a person who has an emotional, romantic and/or sexual orientation towards people of the opposite gender.

Homophobia: the fear or dislike of someone who identifies as lesbian or gay.

Homosexual: this might be considered a more clinical term used to describe someone who has an emotional romantic and/or sexual orientation towards someone of the same gender. The term 'gay' is now more generally used.

Intersex: describes a person who may have the biological attributes of both sexes or whose biological attributes do not fit with societal assumptions about what constitutes male or female. Intersex people can identify as male, female or non-binary.

Lesbian: refers to a woman who has an emotional, romantic and/or sexual orientation towards women.

LGBTQ: the acronym for lesbian, gay, bi and trans and queer.

Non-binary: an umbrella term for a person who does not identify as male or female.

Outed: when a lesbian, gay, bi or trans person's sexual orientation or gender identity is disclosed to someone else without their consent.

Pansexual: refers to a person who is not limited in sexual choice with regard to biological sex, gender or gender identity.

Pronoun: words we use to refer to people's gender in conversation – for example, 'he' or 'she'. Some people may prefer others to refer to them in gender-neutral language, and use pronouns such as 'they'/'their' and 'ze'/'zir'.

Queer: in the past, considered a derogatory term for LGBTQ individuals. The term has now been reclaimed by LGBTQ young people in particular who don't identify with traditional categories around gender identity and sexual orientation, but is still viewed to be derogatory by some.

Questioning: the process of exploring your own sexual orientation and/or gender identity.

Sex: assigned to a person on the basis of primary sex characteristics (genitalia) and reproductive functions. Sometimes the terms 'sex' and 'gender' are interchanged to mean 'male' or 'female'.

Sexual orientation: a person's emotional, romantic and/or sexual attraction to another person.

Trans: an umbrella term to describe people whose gender is not the same as, or does not sit comfortably with, the sex they were assigned at birth. Trans people may describe themselves using one or more of a wide variety of terms, including (but not limited to) transgender, cross-dresser, non-binary, genderqueer (GQ).

Transgender man: a term used to describe someone who is assigned female gender at birth, but identifies and lives as a man. This may be shortened to trans man, or FTM, an abbreviation for female-to-male.

Transgender woman: a term used to describe someone who is assigned male gender at birth, but identifies and lives as a woman. This may be shortened to trans woman, or MTF, an abbreviation for male-to-female.

Transitioning: the steps a trans person may take to live in the gender with which they identify. Each person's transition will involve different things. For some this involves medical intervention, such as hormone therapy and surgeries, but not all trans people want or are able to have this. Transitioning also might involve things such as telling friends and family, dressing differently and changing official documents.

Transphobia: the fear or dislike of someone who identifies as trans.

Transsexual: this was used in the past as a more clinical term (similarly to *homosexual*) to refer to someone who transitioned to live in the 'opposite' gender to the one assigned at birth. This term is still used by some, although many people prefer the term 'trans' or 'transgender'.

So, who are you? In your heart, what is your identity? Imagine feeling that you were born in the wrong body. Perhaps you are feeling that way and you're finding it hard to find someone to connect to? There is a supportive movement out there for those looking to navigate the complicated subject of gender.

I am in awe of the transgender community, and the bravery and commitment of those transforming their lives. In order to truly understand what it's like to be trans, it's important to talk about it and realize that's it wrong to 'freakify' anyone on the planet – it's time to humanize instead.

I interviewed the immensely clever writer **Juno Dawson**, a transgender woman, who was happy to open up on the subject for *Open*.

GC: Do you still feel that there's a problem when it comes to representation of different sorts of people, representing different stories in the media in general? Not just in literature, but when you watch the telly, when you go to the cinema . . .

JD: Yeah, I think it's getting better, I'll definitely say that. And we have to bear in mind that as an LGBT community we are looking at about five per cent of the population. So I guess you'd expect about five per cent of the people you see on the telly and in films to be from the LGBT community . . . I don't think we're there yet. Although we're getting better.

I think reality TV completely changed representation on television of minority groups, in that drama and scripted drama was so white and so straight at the time, but then all of a sudden *Big Brother* started, and clearly they were looking to cast a diverse group. Nadia was, I guess, the first trans woman to feature significantly on British television, and that was now over a decade ago. Really, now, when you look at *EastEnders*, *Coronation Street*, *Hollyoaks*, they are fairly diverse. I think actually if anyone's got a real problem it's Hollywood, where we are still seeing the same ten white heterosexual cisgender actors playing all the roles.

GC: **How are we able to feel more comfortable with chatting about the normalization of LGBT representation?**

JD: It's tough because you constantly get two lots of cries: the sort of man-babies — if you look at the response to *Ghostbusters* for example — 'Oh, there's a gay agenda. There's a trans agenda.' Or, similarly, you get people from within the community saying it's tokenism. So it's really hard to win. But I think being able to humanize groups is really important. We have to get away from this idea that minority groups are a mass of people who will eat and speak exactly the same. Young people seem much more able to take people as individuals . . . It's ridiculous to say that all Muslim people are the same, or that all trans people are the same, or that all gay people are the same. So I think the positive effect of better representation is it humanizes minority groups more, hopefully.

GC: **If you're not trans, but trying to talk about it, it's easy to become fearful of saying the wrong words – calling someone who was a he and now a she, 'he', or vice versa, or not knowing whether to say 'transsexual' or 'transgender', and so on. There are so many different tiers of the unknown for lots of people talking about this sensitive issue, and it does make me worry that it stops people from talking in the first place, and everybody just feels awkward.**

JD: I'm increasingly aware that we have to be able to have conversations, even if they're difficult. I think one of the downsides of social media has been how reactive and angry we can be. I don't think that trans people should have to debate their existence. I've just, this very week, written an article which is 'The Dos and Don'ts of Asking Trans People Questions'. It's interesting because no white, straight, cisgender man is having to answer questions about what it's like to be a white, straight, cisgender man. But trans representation and trans visibility is so new, and if I'm willing to be out there as a trans woman I am up for answering questions.

You've just got to keep it polite and keep it sane. Would you be asking about your gran's genitals? Would you be asking your gran, 'Do you still sleep with men, or do you sleep with women? What surgeries will you have?' If people come to you with sane questions, even if it's a misconception — like a really common one is, 'Did you used to be a drag queen?' — I'm like, 'Well, no, but I will now explain to you the difference between a performance drag artist and me: the drag artist is being paid. I am not being paid every day to dress like this.'

GC: How different is life as Juno in comparison to James? What does the world look like now? Do you face different things day to day, or is it quite similar – you just feel more naturally aligned?

JD: Alignment's a really good word. It's funny because in a spiritual — I hate the word 'spiritual' — kind of inner-world way, everything feels very calm and feels very right. I make a lot more sense; my relationships make a lot more sense. Though on a practical level things are a lot harder right now. It's a lot harder to be a woman — you have pressure to look a certain way, to make a lot more effort. I have to get up earlier to get ready, make extra time for leg shaving, extra time for armpit shaving, all of those practical issues that come along with being a woman that I think cisgender women have been doing so long — since they were twelve/thirteen — that actually they forget it's bullshit, and they forget that men are not doing this. So on a practical level it's harder — people stare and people mutter about me, people point me out, people say, 'Oh, that's a man.' I've made things a bit harder for myself, but spiritually I feel better than I've ever felt, and things make a lot more sense.

GC: **When trying to understand the trans experience more broadly, it's important to remember that everyone's different, right?**

JD: There are as many ways to be transgender as there are trans people. I am what the kids would call 'binary transgender': I was born physically male, but now I am one hundred per cent convinced I am a woman; I've always been a woman. I want to be called 'she'. My passport now says I'm a woman; my birth certificate will eventually say I'm a woman. For some people it's not that easy — they prefer 'non-binary' or 'gender queer', or 'gender fluid'. But I think the advice that I would give, and I give this advice to young adults who write to me, is be patient, because these things really do take time. There really isn't a rush.

Also, I would say, as pure practical advice (although this is just advice for the UK), do get yourself on a waiting list, because actually waiting lists are so long that that's your thinking time. So I'd almost doubled up on thinking space, because I did two years of thinking time before I even got on a waiting list. Just don't rush things. That's good advice for dealing with your family as well; just because you've been thinking about this for a year and a half, you can't dump it on your parents and expect them to be fine with it in a fortnight.

There is no quick way to transition. I think I've had to learn patience — I was very impatient. And I would say that if you're going to start thinking about gender transition in any regard, really, it's to start thinking about patience first, and understanding that you are in it for the long haul. Because another one of those slightly daft questions that trans people get asked all the time is, 'When will you be finished?' — and actually you're never finished. You're not baking a cake; you're going to be living with your gender identity until you die. So getting patience from day one isn't bad advice, I don't think.

Also, and I think this will chime with younger readers, it doesn't need to be a big deal. When I was in my early twenties, I was in a band — who wasn't? — an electro-punk band, and looking back there was a real trans element to it. I was wearing fur coats, leather pants, stockings and suspenders, and it was pure performance — I wasn't going to Tesco like that. When I look at younger people now, there's more of an element of experimenting with gender — 'Yeah, I'm a girl, but I can wear a suit if I want, I can wear a bowler hat if I want, it's just me playing with fashion, it's me playing with my identity, and it's not permanent.'

That's the other thing with gender — you're not carving it in stone. It is a very sort of hysterical way of looking at transgenderism to think, 'Oh my God, it's this irreversible change. Last week she decided she was trans, so now she's in hospital having surgery.' It really doesn't work like that. I was really proud of Eddie Izzard when he said, 'I'm transgender' — because of course he is — he's playing with hair, clothes and make-up, which is 'gender'. So the word 'transsexual' has weirdly gone out of fashion, but I'm really proud to be a transsexual in that I am, through various medical interventions, now seeking to change my sex.

GC: How did your parents take it?

JD: Yeah they were good, but they weren't good overnight. I would say there was a definite period where I think my mum in particular thought I was putting myself through hardship, and exposing myself to danger. And, statistically, she is right. I am more vulnerable as a trans woman than I was as a gay man — but then you can only panic for so long. The real surprise was my dad . . . Given that I've not had a great relationship with him, I thought this could be the end. But actually it's made our relationship better, and I think that was because he was trying to make a relationship happen with a son, and he never really had a son . . . He's always got on much better with my sister, because I think he understood how to make a father—daughter relationship work, and now he's just acquired another daughter. So actually we've been getting along better than we have in a really long time. All's well that ends well.

When you're dealing with a relationship with a parent, it feels like there's a lot on the line, like you're really gambling with something special, but it did have to be done. It felt a bit like going to the gallows or something — I got the train up from Leeds and I was like [groans]. I think again it's very much about patience and understanding. As much as you're like, 'Ugh, why can't you be fine with this?' you owe them some time as well, because you've had a lot of time.

GC: Do you have any good advice in terms of people to seek out, to google, that have really great opinions or really great experiences on being trans?

194

JD : There's Gendered Intelligence — Gendered Intelligence is a wonderful charity who support both trans people and their parents. There's Mermaids, another charity who particularly support the parents of trans young people. In terms of my personal role models, for me it was about finding trans people who were my age, I think, more than anything. I was looking up to people like Paris Lees, Andreja Pejić, and I read Juliet Jacques's memoir, which is called *Trans: A Memoir*, which is brilliant. So it's about sort of finding people that chime with you, because there isn't one way to be trans. So not all trans people will necessarily inspire you. I disagree with most of what Caitlyn Jenner says, but I'm still very relieved she exists, because she puts her trans views on a platform that we wouldn't have had otherwise. So I don't agree with her on a political level, but at the same time I really respect everything she's done in terms of being so out there and so open about her gender.

GC : **Do you think the internet has elevated the trans rights movement?**

JD : Now we've all become sort of experts — the internet has very much democratized freedom of speech in that we all have the same platform now. Before it was the media — the media was in charge of picking people out and saying, 'Her face fits,' or, 'His face fits, so we'll get that person on TV,' and they were very much selected. One of the things I like about the internet is that it has, by default, become more diverse, because we choose who we want to listen to.

But the problem is it's about filtering in or out those people that we think we relate to, I guess, and understanding that a lot of the time these experts that we're seeing on the internet don't necessarily have any qualifications whatsoever. I guess it's about finding those people whose beliefs, politics, faith, most align with yours. But I'm also a big, big believer in 'Turn the computer off and go walk in nature' — you have to have real conversations, and you have to have conversations with people who don't agree with one hundred per cent of the things you say, because if you're in an echo chamber you're not going to be changing anybody's hearts or minds. That's the danger with the internet — because we can select just what we want to hear, and we can convince ourselves that this is the world we're living in. Almost, it's become virtual reality. You have to actually go out and live in the world, with all its problems, with its homophobia and transphobia and racism, otherwise you're living inside a palace of your own creation, and I don't think it's healthy.

 What would you say to those who inflict prejudice on the LGBT community?

JD: There have always been transgender people; there have always been LGBT people; there have always been women; there have always been people who are trying to hark back to this 'golden age' that didn't really exist. We're not trying to take anything away from white, cisgender, heterosexual men. I don't want them to lose rights — we're just asking for the same rights. You're not under attack; we're just catching up.

SEXUAL HEALTH

197

If we're gonna do it, let's do it healthily

Through working on a campaign called When It's On, It's On with Durex (the condom brand), I discovered an alarming new attitude when it comes to our sexual health. A kind of 'invincibility culture' has emerged amongst some young people, and their attitude towards sexually transmitted infections has changed dramatically, stopping many of them from taking the right precautions when it comes to having safe sex. Shockingly, forty per cent of sexually active teens admitted to having sex with more than one person WITHOUT A CONDOM.

Increasingly, young people seem to have the idea that most STIs, such as chlamydia, just aren't that serious and can easily be cleared up with a 'pill'. Even more worrying, almost half of those surveyed said that contracting HIV isn't something that would happen to them or any of their friends. Meanwhile, the numbers of young people catching STIs is on the UP. You do the maths!

On the bright side, the survey also found that whilst over a third of guys in straight, sexually active couples will sometimes try to get away with not using a condom, loads of others actually say it's a turn on when a woman has the confidence to insist on it, in the heat of the moment. Unsafe sex needs to be a deal breaker!

Yes, there is lots out there in the way of birth control, but the only effective way of preventing pregnancy AND STIs is by arming yourself with things that you can buy easily from a chemist, or a corner shop, a twenty-four-hour petrol station, or even a nightclub: CONDOMS. And yet there is still a needless self-conscious attitude towards getting hold of these marvels.

It seems it's not just teens who are too embarrassed to talk about condoms – or to find out where they can get them for free – even grown-ups have given up on talking to young people about safe sex. Perhaps our growing culture of sexualization amongst teens and increasingly easy access to porn terrifies the grown-ups so much they don't want to break it down and chat about the basics.

This means that everyone is kind of walking around in a horny fog, googling more and more info rather than verbalizing, shooting the breeze or asking trusted experts for the facts.

This time round, I'm begging you to sit up and listen. The fact is that the I-just-use-the-pull-out technique nonsense approach to sex means STIs are on the up. Yep. Gremlins are trying to party on our privates. I know – I sound like a bonkers supply teacher in a sex-ed lesson, but it's true . . . We need to inspire a more positive and confident approach towards safe sex. Fill your back pockets with rubbers.*

Whenever I ask anyone of school age about what sex education they receive, I'm alarmed to nearly ALWAYS hear that the sex education in their school is pretty non-connective or non-existent. Where is education going wrong?

*VIMN Ad & Brand Solutions Insight with Tapestry Research. Base: 1,641; P16-24.

Winkle Toplines Report, 2015. Beliefs, Insight & Reason-to-Believe screener in the UK, France and Italy. P11.

WHAT DO THE
EXPERTS SAY?

For thirteen years, Kelly Abbot worked in a pupil referral unit with vulnerable young people in Years 10 and 11, so aged fifteen to sixteen, most of whom were from socially excluded families. Kelly's focus was on sexual health and relationships.

You have to . . . break down those barriers . . . It's not like I was teaching anyone how to do sexual acts. But you cannot turn a blind eye to the fact that we know some young people are already engaging in intimacy, whether it's giving 'hand jobs' or 'blowjobs' or whatever, to full-blown sex. My approach was to desensitize. I'd say, 'You tell me every word that you know for your privates, and then write them up on the whiteboard. There were things I'd never even heard of. I can't go into a classroom and say, 'This is the vagina, these are the labia, and this is the penis.' Some kids don't know what the labia are.

What should sex be taught as? It should be taught as a physical, intimate connection between two people who are emotionally able to deal with the energy that sex generates. We all get to an age when you get tingling sensations — that's human nature. But if you're having those tinglings in your pants, and no one is giving you information at home — like a lot of the young people I was teaching — then some seek sexual contact from their peers. Schools and parents need to be aware of this and the fact that there is the wrong self-education happening out there. What young people aren't getting in schools they are trying to find online instead, a lot of it via porn, which is not a true reflection of real sex whatsoever.

CONTRACEPTION

If you are under the age of eighteen and are thinking of becoming sexually active, then you need to have a conversation with your GP or local sexual health clinic to discuss how to protect yourself. Your doctor can advise on the right kind of contraception for you, and if necessary talk about any issues around each method and why you need it.

NAVIGATING THE MIND BOGGLE OF SAFE SEX

I'm gonna start with the fact that the only method of contraception that protects you against nearly all sexually transmitted infections and unwanted pregnancy is a CONDOM. (FYI: if used correctly and consistently it is ninety-eight per cent effective at protecting against unwanted pregnancy, HIV and AIDS, gonorrhoea and chlamydia – definitions on pages 207–8). Yep, a good old, trusty 'rubber johnny', sheath or 'French letter' as your granny might call it (a term that originates from the seventeenth century) or perhaps 'penis hat' as they are sometimes described in Nigeria, or 'love and necessity' in South Korea, or 'safety tool' in Hungary.

(See more detailed benefits on 'penis hats' on pages 198–9.)

I'm for a condom above anything. It's got yer back from many perspectives.

When it comes to heading to the sexual health clinic or going to speak to your GP about contraception, speak UP. Ask doctors questions. Remember, they **DO NOT JUDGE** their patients, and see many, many, many different people, each with a different story.

LET'S GET REAL

It goes without saying that nobody's up for an 'unwanted' pregnancy. So there are lots of ways to prevent getting preggo, though the pill and condoms are the most popular, other methods are referred to as contraception too. It's important to know all your options and choose the one that is right for you.

WHICH KIND OF CONTRACEPTION SHOULD I USE?

There are fifteen different methods of 'birth control' contraception currently available in the UK. The type that works best for you will depend on your health and circumstances, and some are more effective than others. The most widely used forms of contraception in the UK are condoms, followed by the contraceptive pill.

We asked the **Brook Advisory Centre** to provide us with definitions of the types available to younger people:

- **Long active reversible contraceptives** – they do what it says, they last a long time once they are inserted (so you can forget about them) and when you want to get pregnant or stop using them you can get them removed. They are the most effective methods of contraception – over ninety-nine per cent effective – and they include:

    - **Contraceptive implant**

    - **Intra-uterine system, or IUS**

    - **Intra-uterine device or IUD**

    - **Contraceptive injection**

There are other types of contraceptive methods that you need to remember when to take or use. These include:

- **Combined contraceptive pill**
- **Progesterone-only contraceptive pill**
- **Contraceptive patch**
- **Vaginal ring**
- **Male condom**
- **Female condom**
- **Diaphragm**
- **Cap**

Important **Forgetting to take or use these methods is a common reason for them failing to protect against pregnancy.**

Note that if you are taking one form of contraception you can double up by wearing a condom. And, I REPEAT, the ONLY thing that can protect you from a number of STIs is a CONDOM.

AMAZING!!

The good news is that there is a scheme that gives out free condoms to those aged thirteen to twenty-four. QUICK, go type 'free condoms' into Google and you will find your local scheme. There you can type in your postcode and it'll tell you how you can get yours. There really is NO excuse not to take advantage of this!

NO NAMES. NO JUDGEMENTS. NO WORRIES.

If you have had unprotected sex (that is sex without using contraception) or think that your contraception might have failed, you can use **emergency contraception**. There are different options:

- **Emergency contraceptive pill**. There are two different types:

   1) Levonorgestrel (Levonelle) can be taken within taken three days (seventy-two hours) after unprotected sex

   2) Ulipristal Acetate (ellaOne) can be taken five days (120 hours) after unprotected sex.

   These methods will be more effective the sooner they are taken after unprotected sex.

- **Emergency intra-uterine device** (IUD). A small plastic and copper device that can be fitted in your uterus up to five days (120 hours) after unprotected sex. You can choose to keep using the IUD as your regular method of contraception or get it removed during your next period.

There are some brilliant expert websites that will tell you more about contraception, including the **Brook Advisory Centre** mentioned previously and also the ever flabbergastingly amazing **NHS** and the **Family Planning Association**. I don't say it lightly when I say advice is essential when you start having sex. It is some of the most important information you will ever learn.

Young people's contraceptive clinics via the NHS are also a great place to seek unbiased support and do a pregnancy test if there is a worry. A pregnancy test is usually accurate three weeks after the last time you had unprotected sex.

YOU'VE GOT OPTIONS

If you are pregnant and if you are less than twenty-four weeks pregnant (a doctor can tell you how far along you are) there are three options available to you, and you have the right to choose any one of them:

- Continuing the pregnancy and raising the child
- Continuing the pregnancy and placing the child for adoption
- Ending the pregnancy by having an abortion

ABORTION

Abortion is the medical process of ending a pregnancy – and is also known as a termination. A pregnancy is ended either by taking medication, or having a minor surgical procedure; this often depends on how far along in your pregnancy you are. Most abortions in England, Wales and Scotland are carried out before twenty-four weeks of pregnancy (calculated from the first day of your last period). Abortion is not legal in the Republic of Ireland or Northern Ireland. They can be carried out after twenty-four weeks in certain circumstances, but they are simpler and safer the earlier they are carried out.

Unwanted pregnancy is definitely something you need to be aware of. One in three women in the UK will have an abortion by the time they are forty-five years old. Though teenage pregnancy has been significantly reduced over the past decade, there is some risk of pregnancy even if you haven't started your periods yet, and sex just once can lead to a pregnancy if no contraception is used.

If you do become pregnant and it is not planned or wanted, your GP and sexual health/abortion clinics are there to help you deal with your situation and talk through the choices with you to help you decide whether or not to have an abortion.

Where can I go if I am thinking of or want an abortion?
You can get help in deciding on whether to have an abortion by contacting:

> The British Pregnancy Advisory Service (BPAS)
>
> Marie Stopes UK
>
> The National Unplanned Pregnancy Advisory Service (NUPAS)
>
> A contraception or family planning clinic, sexual health clinic or genitourinary medicine clinic
>
> Your doctor and ask for a referral

Where is the abortion performed and how long do I have to wait for an appointment?
Abortions can only be carried out in an NHS hospital or a licensed clinic – nowhere else.

Waiting times vary, but you shouldn't have to wait more than two weeks for your initial appointment to discuss having an abortion. Abortions can also be performed in private licensed clinics, and your doctor can refer you to one if you choose to pay for an abortion.

Can I get an abortion at any time during my pregnancy?
It is legal to have an abortion up to twenty-four weeks into a pregnancy in the UK. After this date there must be very specific circumstances, such as danger to the mother's life.

How can I tell how many weeks pregnant I am?
Your doctor will ask you when the first day of your last period was and then calculate from that day. You will also need an ultrasound scan to confirm the exact date. This is particularly important if you have irregular periods, and these happen for lots of reasons – some people can even get pregnant without having a period as they may still ovulate (produce an egg) before a first period happens. And also things like exam stress can make periods irregular.

What if I am confused and don't know whether I want an abortion?
The decision to have an abortion is yours and yours alone: only you can make it. But when you seek help you will be told of your options (one of which is going through with your pregnancy) and offered impartial counselling and support to help you decide. It is also important, if you feel that you can, to talk to your parents who will help you think it through. It's one of the most important decisions you will ever make and may well be an emotionally difficult time too. Your family and people who love you are often invaluable in providing support, but if you don't feel you can talk to your parents – if you have an unstable or difficult relationship with them, for example – then seek out trusted friends and other adults, including your local GP or practice nurse. You should not feel in any way pressured into having an abortion or be made to feel ashamed or guilty by anyone.

STIs

OH, and apologies in advance, but this is what we're waging war on by doing our best to keep safe and by using a condom.

You may think that you don't need to worry about sexually transmitted infections, but you do: never be casual about sexual health. Do ask your partner questions about their sexual history and always make sure you're as safe as you can be. An STI, or sexually transmitted infection, is basically any kind of bacterial or viral infection that can be passed on through unprotected sexual contact. It doesn't matter how many times you've had sex or how many partners you've had; anyone can get an STI.

Pay attention to your body and do get anything that is unusual for you checked out, especially if it itches, has come up in a rash or there is unusual discharge. If you don't want to go to your GP – though they have seen everything and will keep it confidential – there are lots of walk-in clinics that you can go to. It is common to feel nervous about getting tested but don't worry – most infections are easily treated. You can find out more information at the Brook Advisory website: www.brook.org.uk

CHLAMYDIA

The most common bacterial STI is chlamydia. Up to fifty pre cent of girls with chlamydia don't have any symptoms but if left untreated it can have serious consequences, such as pelvic inflammatory disease (PID) and infertility, which means it is important for young people to get tested if they have had unprotected sex, and by that I mean if a condom has not been used. From recent statistics, chlamydia is found in around three per cent of both males and females aged sixteen to twenty-four. Chlamydia is treatable with antibiotics, and it is easy to get tested at your local GP surgery or at a sexual health clinic.

207

GENITAL HERPES

Genital herpes is a common infection caused by the herpes simplex virus (HSV). It causes painful blisters on the genitals and the surrounding areas. It is a chronic – long term – condition. It will remain in your body and intermittently become activated – up to four or five times a year in the first two years after infection, though over time it will become less frequent, and less severe.

GONORRHOEA

Gonorrhoea is quite rare – with an estimated less than one in 1,000 people in the UK having it, but it is on the rise, particularly amongst gay males. Like chlamydia, it can be treated with antibiotics and it is easily tested for by a GP or at a clinic.

HIV

Human immunodeficiency virus (HIV) tends not to show symptoms at first, other than early on when it often presents as a flu-like illness within a few weeks of infection that will in all likelihood be passed off as a simple cold virus. Around seventeen per cent of those who have HIV are unaware of their infection, and so at risk of unknowingly passing it on to a sexual partner. There is no cure for HIV/AIDS, but if it is found early it can be treated by antiretroviral therapy effectively. The longer it is left, the less effective the treatment. Around two in 1,000 people in the UK are living with HIV and it predominantly affects gay men and those of African ethnicity.

HPV

HPV is a group of viruses, some of which cause genital warts, and some types can result in cervical cancer, though for most people the virus will go away on its own within a year, without causing serious health problems. Since the introduction of the highly effective HPV vaccine, which is now given to girls aged twelve to thirteen, the likelihood of girls and young women contracting HPV has now been significantly reduced. Before the vaccination programme, around one in six women had a high risk of developing HPV, and in young women the risk was higher, with a quarter of women aged eighteen to twenty-four developing it.

PUBIC LICE

Pubic lice have nothing to do with poor hygiene. They are tiny parasitic insects that live in coarse body hair, such as pubic hair, but not in the hair on your head. They are yellow-grey in colour, about 2mm long and have a crab-like appearance, hence the common term for them of 'crabs'. Symptoms range from itching in affected areas, black powdery droppings in your underwear, brownish eggs in pubic or other body hair and either tiny sky-blue spots or blood spots on the skin. A sexual health clinic or your GP can easily diagnose pubic lice.

SYPHILIS

Syphilis is a chronic bacterial disease that is contracted chiefly by infection during sex and is relatively rare amongst STIs. Symptoms of syphilis can include: mouth sores, usually within two to three weeks after contracting the disease; and sores on the body – but mainly on the vulva (the lips around the opening to the vagina), the clitoris, the cervix and around the opening to the urethra (the opening to the urinary tract) and the anus.

CYSTITIS

Cystitis is not an STI, but sex can trigger it. It is usually caused by bacteria irritating the bladder lining and a common symptom is pain when you wee.

WHAT DO YOU KNOW ABOUT PRIVATE PARTS?

Don't know about you, but I couldn't label *every* part of my vulva. So I thought we could all take the test!

Have a go at labelling below what you think the parts are . . .

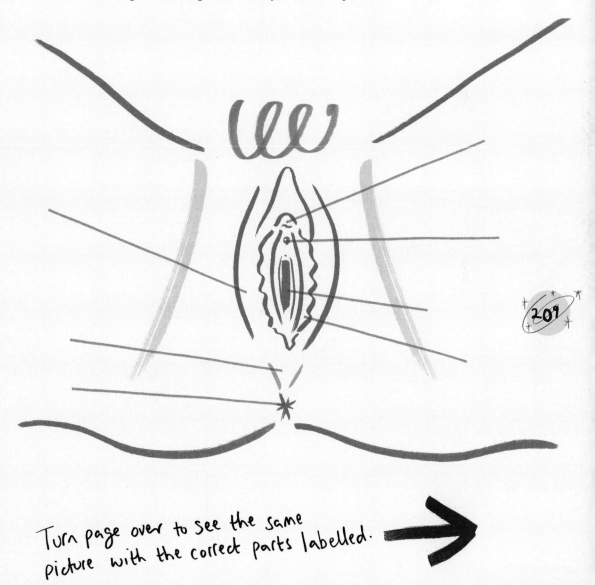

209

Turn page over to see the same picture with the correct parts labelled. ➜

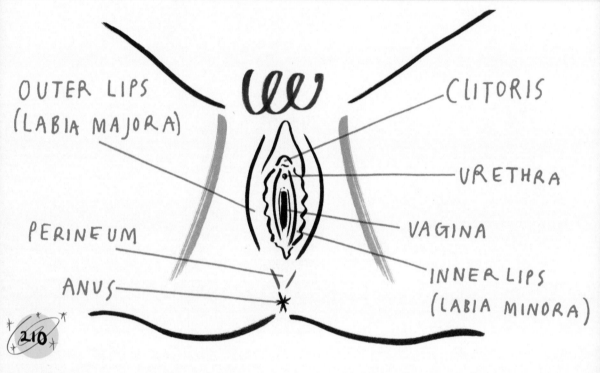

OUTER LIPS
(LABIA MAJORA)

CLITORIS

URETHRA

PERINEUM

VAGINA

ANUS

INNER LIPS
(LABIA MINORA)

210

MASTURBATION

This is one of the most private, private things you can do, if you choose to, alone.

No one talks about it, but lots of people do it. It may be a little bit of a secret, but it's not a bad one. If you touch yourself for pleasure, it ain't nothing to be ashamed of: you are normal.

It's different strokes for different folks; everyone has their own way of doing it.

You are allowed to be inquisitive about sex and have fantasies.

Masturbation WILL NOT make you pregnant or ill.

It is not, I repeat NOT, bad for your health.

Thank goodnessssssss!

PORN

212

THREE IMPORTANT THINGS
TO REMEMBER . . . .

1. You cannot unsee things

It is important, if you decide to access porn, to make sure you don't upset yourself by being led down the wrong path. There's an incredibly foggy land of porn out there, and just because it is accessible doesn't mean it is right for us all to view. The wrong kind of porn or too much porn can affect our real lives when it goes beyond fantasy, and it can lead to both addiction and intimacy issues. Trust your gut – if you feel like something isn't quite right in some way or disturbs you, never forget that the power of the OFF button is yours. And never forget the power of your own imagination alone when it comes to sexual fantasy. It's within your control, and it is so much better.

2. It is unrealistic

The positions, the bodies, the scenarios, the pleasure portrayed in porn is not true to real life. Real sex is messier, hairier, more awkward and therefore way more fun! Real sex usually involves two people who either really love or fancy each other. There are all sorts of emotions and noises to discover that are not represented in porn. In porn, it's an actor's job to pretend and to fit into a hyper-sexualized context, because the porn industry makes major bucks that way, not because the porn stars know something we don't. If you are going to watch it, then that's your choice. Don't demonize yourself . . . but DO protect yourself by knowing that it's worlds away from what it's really like to have sex. You can't expect real-life sex to represent anything you see in porn.

3. It is possible to get addicted*

It is very easy to get addicted to the short, sharp hit porn can give you. As with everything we do, moderation is key. Always assess whether it's making you feel bad or guilty, or whether you can't get it off your mind.

*Go to the ADDICTION test on page 94.

If you are worried that someone you know is too into porn, and it's affecting them, speak to them calmly and explain your concerns. Even if it's embarrassing. They may not realize that it's the porn that is affecting their behaviour.

Please refer to organizations at the back of this book for extra help on porn addiction and educating ourselves on the porn phenomenon.

CONSENT, RAPE AND RAPE CULTURE

In the eyes of the law, if someone doesn't consent to a sexual act, then it's a criminal offence to have sex with them. No grey area: if one person doesn't want to do it, IT SHOULDN'T HAPPEN. And if you are under sixteen, and have felt intimidated into saying yes, or not saying no, to sex – but did not want it to happen – it is rape.

This is regardless of how intoxicated someone might be, regardless of what someone might be wearing, regardless of what's happened up until the moment they decide they don't want to. I know lots of girls and women live with a fear of sexual violence lurking in the shadows, for the simple reason that men are physically stronger. This DOES NOT mean that it doesn't happen to men too, though.

Consent, rape and rape culture are the most complex issues I've ever had to cover on the Radio 1 *Surgery* show. It's so important that we all know what rape is, and what to do if it happens to us or one of our friends. It is too important to ignore. It is a taboo subject, and that's because it's a hard and scary subject. But that doesn't mean we shouldn't talk about it.

I spoke to a brave and inspiring young woman who had been a victim of sexual violence about what she wishes she had more information about when it happened to her. The following interview contains descriptions of an upsetting and graphic nature, and may be triggering if you've experienced sexual violence. If you want to skip it, that's OK.

GC: Do you consider yourself a victim? Is it something that kind of forms part of you?

A: I think that was one of the biggest things that bothered me afterwards in terms of all the literature you get given, and every system that you have to go through for various aspects. They always refer to you as 'victim'. Again, from my personal experience, that just brings out the loss of control and power over your own body and over your own being. In my view, it basically gives that little bit more, again, to both the perpetrator and also to other people, which, following something like rape, is the last thing that you want.

You read these pamphlets and booklets, everything you get given, but no one knows exactly how someone is going to react. There are moments that are like riding a rollercoaster, at least at first it was very much about trying not to think about it. After weeks I'd wake up and I'd be able to get up and brush my teeth, and I wouldn't have thought about it until then. Those periods get longer and longer, until you make it through an entire morning.

There are times when I can make it through two days, but, there's always the potential for something to trigger it back. And it can be the most innocuous, tiniest little thing that has happened before and hasn't triggered it, but for whatever reason, it does [this time], and it just brings you right back. That can happen at any point.

I was at a work event last November — it was a fancy-dress party thing — I had a glass of Prosecco, and I went to drop off my empty glass, and . . . I smelt the same aftershave that the person that raped me had been wearing. It's a very common aftershave — you smell it on the tube, you smell it in the office, you smell it in shops, pubs, everywhere — but, for whatever reason, that just brought me right back straight away. It's little things like that. I don't think it's something that you can ever truly get over while there are still triggers that will still bring you straight back.

GC: Why do you think it's important for people to report sexual abuse, assault and violence of all forms?

A: I think, for me, the biggest thing was that I don't think I could've lived with myself if I found out that he'd done the same thing to someone else. I didn't want that guilt and that burden and that worry. I think, as hard as going through a case is, the outcome, in the sense that — not that I'd done my bit, or even that I'd stopped them doing it again — it is a weight off my mind in terms of I haven't got that constant fear of a knock on the door or a call from someone at the Met Sapphire unit . . . to ask me the question, 'Do [you] want to pursue it now?' It's done and dusted. I think the fact that I know that he's off the streets is good . . . There is no sentence that could've been passed down by the courts that would ever make up for what happened to me. I've got something that will affect me for the rest of my life, and it makes certain aspects of my life very difficult — relationships, trusting people . . .

GC: What about all the stuff that's in the news about people that don't get sentenced properly?

A: I don't think it's a perfect system. I also don't think that just locking someone up for twenty years is going to cause any real good in the long run. I think there needs to be a lot more in terms of rehabilitation of offenders. People coming in and out of prison is just getting bigger and bigger, and it's almost a self-fulfilling prophecy in the fact that it then means there's less resources to help rehabilitation, which then just makes the problem worse because you get more people going back in.

GC: Would you have any advice for people that know someone who has experienced sexual violence, in terms of how they should speak to them about it, or if they should at all?

A: Just be there. I told my best friend, and she came round and she brought a bottle of wine and some kind of fizzy grape juice — non-alcoholic thing — because she wasn't sure if I'd want to drink or not, and she brought some ice cream and some fruit, because she wasn't sure if I wanted to eat junk food or eat fruit. She tried to cover all bases, and it actually injected a little bit of humour into the situation . . . Yeah, it was just — it was being there. And we started watching *Ab Fab* or something, and then I did start to open up and talk a little bit. She was just there to . . . listen. I'd probably say don't ask questions . . . Just be there to listen and just digest what they say.

219

GC: Has there been any organization, or online portal, or support group that you would recommend that has been particularly helpful?

A: As soon as possible after it happens, I would highly recommend the Havens — these are centres across London (other similar organizations exist around the country) — they're completely anonymous and basically you can get forensics taken that are then stored, that then if you wanted to pursue a case later on, you do have that option available, which, if you don't do that, it can make things incredibly difficult. They in no way put any pressure on you to report it, or not report it — they just store this on file. And they can also, if you want them to for forensic purposes, store your clothing.

They also can arrange counselling if you want. They have on-site counsellors. I know that you can do that through them, and they're a service that will assist you for the first year.

They have got a proper dedicated medical team, and in my case my rape was quite violent, and they were able to deal with my other medical needs at the time as well, which meant that I didn't have to go through A&E or anything, which . . . just that kind of peace and quiet was very helpful, and also not having to see various different doctors and nurses, just kind of be looked after by one doctor and a nurse was helpful for me.

GC: Societally, do you feel like there needs to be a shift in our attitude towards rape?

A: I definitely became more in tune with certain things . . . There are an awful lot of jokes that are made about rape that I think we're almost used to because of similar 'banter' — it's like we've almost tuned out of how awful they are, because we do hear them quite a lot . . .

As a society we seem to think it's OK to joke about that kind of thing. The one that always gets me every time is, 'It's not rape if you shout "surprise".'

As far as I'm concerned, there is no grey area, there are no blurred lines: someone either consents to sex or they don't. There is no grey area or miscommunication. I don't care how many drinks or dinners or whatever you've bought someone, and I don't care if they've happily gone up to your flat, or invited you in and got into bed and are halfway through — as soon as they turn around and say no, that means no.

GC: **What about advice for those in a relationship with someone who has experienced sexual violence or assault — what would you say?**

A: Relationships are difficult. There's going to be a whole range of emotions. With me, there was a complete lack of trust . . . I really wanted to open up and trust, and I found it incredibly difficult. I think just be there, again, listen, be guided by the other person. As human beings, we're almost pre-designed to be selfish and self-centred and think everything is because of something we've done. This is certainly much bigger than that. Just because something was fine last week, don't assume it's going to be fine this week. It took me the best part of three years to even get into a position where I was prepared to have a relationship with somebody, and I still find sex very difficult. Again, there is support out there. There are groups that meet, and you can decide whether you want to discuss various things. I know a lot of people have got a lot of help from that.

My Body Back is a project that specializes in supporting those who've experienced sexual violence and assault. Their site features an in-depth list of their services, and a clear list of the different charities dealing with various related issues, regardless of where you are in the UK, or what your particular experience is – from LGBTQ specialists to prevention of forced arranged marriages.

Head to www.mybodybackproject.com

There are also more organizations listed at the back of the book that can help.

FINALLY

Be gentle and patient with yourself and give yourself the time to work out the inner rhythms of your body and soul, whether it's the *boom*, *boom* of a loud giant drum, or a rain-like patter on a bongo. As you evolve and grow, these rhythms will become more layered, like an orchestra. It takes time to feel comfortable with that, and to learn to accept it: stay OPEN and your journey to understanding your individual body and soul can be as exhilarating as it is exhausting.

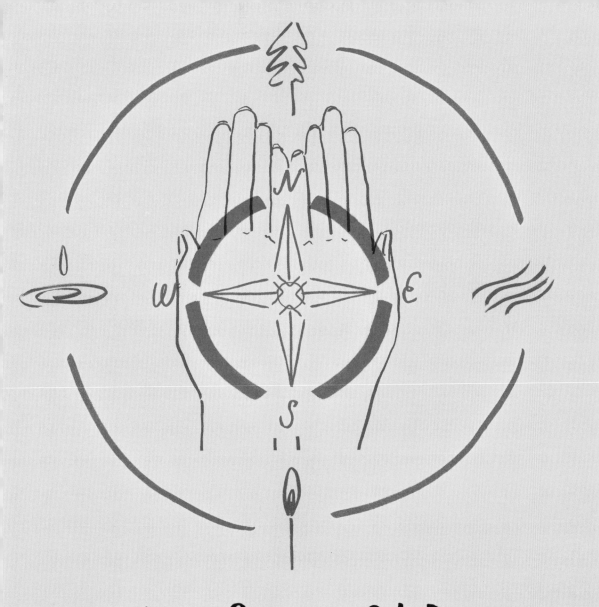

YOUR WORLD

AND

YOUR FUTURE

INTRODUCTION

Think about the world – your globe. Picture it in your head: its roundness – the swirls of delicious greens and blues of the land and seas and oceans. Think about those continents you learn about in geography lessons – how they become so easily identifiable from their beautiful shapes. Think about all the islands in their thousands and thousands. Think about how BIG the world is – all the places you've been, and all the places you would like to see in the future.

Now think about you. Where are you on that globe right now, while you're reading these words?

This part of *Open* looks at what it means to be a human being, to see what's important about it, what's sad about it, what's truly joyful about it. And how, even though we only physically occupy the tiniest little patch of the world at any given time, we can add something HUGE to it . . . We can add boundless love and hope, in an infinite number of ways.

The world is EXTRAORDINARY. It can sometimes be gut-sickeningly sad and terrifying, but it's also ridiculously fun and boldly beautiful . . . EXTRAORDINARY. Your world is your future.

224

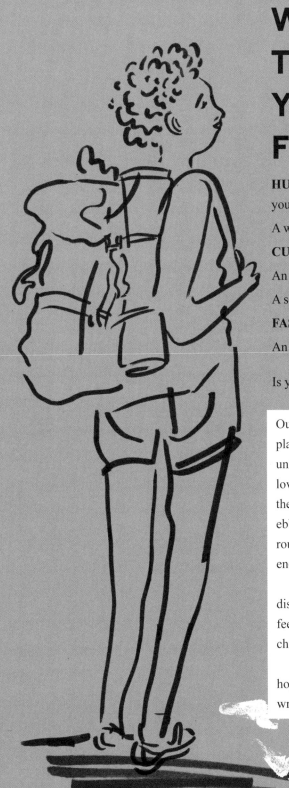

WHAT YOU NEED TO PACK IN YOUR RUCKSACK FOR THIS TRIP

HUMILITY – the ability to be humble and leave your vanity at the door.

A willingness to **LISTEN**.

CURIOSITY and the confidence to ask questions.

An understanding of **ACTIVISM** over **ANGER**.

A sense of **WONDER** for nature.

FASCINATION and bewilderment combined.

An **OPEN** heart and **OPEN** mind.

Is your bag packed? LET'S GO...

Our world can sometimes seem like an overwhelming place to be: sometimes scary, sometimes bleak, often unfair. But with every low there is a high. To understand love, you must understand the opposite; to enjoy the sun, there must be shade. But even when we feel at our lowest ebb, there are never-ending, awe-inspiring experiences round every corner if we find a way to tap into our great energy reserves and just get out there and find them.

One of our biggest problems with the world is how disconnected we sometimes feel from it. It is hard to feel rooted to a general environment that is constantly changing and sometimes feels out of our control.

But it's not out of our control: we have a voice, hopes and dreams, and a sense of what's right and wrong . . . Please keep going.

POLITICS

Politics in the UK can seem like a lot of boring posh people shouting at each other in the House of Commons – that big, dark, heavy room, void of all natural light, with its gloomy green leather-clad seats, and its opulent, Gothic architecture. It is all too easy for the heckles, the angry faces and the strange language to make politics feel difficult to understand, hard to connect to and too remote from the reality of our day-to-day lives – as though it has no relevance.

But it does . . . It REALLY does. A lot of what politicians and the government are deciding now, the laws they are putting in place, will affect your future – your livelihood, your ability to buy a house, even your access to a functioning health service.

I will never, ever forget being lucky enough to be shown round the chamber of the House of Commons by an MP. He scurried about excitedly, as though he was showing off his impressive gaff on MTV *Cribs*! (Anyone remember that show? It basically gave us a peek round super-famous people's insane houses. Google 'Mariah Carey Cribs' to watch a classic episode.) I bought a bottle of 'House of Commons' – branded champagne for twenty-five quid from the gift shop – because I thought it was ludicrous that it existed – and marvelled at the colossal size of everything.

As I walked around, I was moved to think of the brave ones in this world. I bowed my head at a plaque dedicated to Nelson Mandela in Westminster Hall; and I thought of the many young women before me who dedicated their lives to fighting for women to gain the right to vote. Women like Emily Wilding Davison (who allegedly once hid in a crypt in the very burrows we were being shown around), who, in June 1913, was struck when she walked out in front of the King's horse during the Epsom Derby race to draw attention to the seriousness of the suffragette movement, and later died in hospital from her injuries (it is still unknown whether it was intended martyrdom).

I was shown the chambers where MPs go when they have to make big decisions about the laws of the land. My guide told me that one particularly momentous day of parliamentary decision-making was when MPs decided on the legal maximum number of weeks at which a woman should still be permitted to have an abortion. It was at that moment it truly struck – like lightning – just how much power this lot has in all our lives . . . right down to the things that feel the most intense and most personal.

You have to be eighteen years old in this country to be able to vote, but it's never too early to start learning more about politics and how you can get involved as you get closer to voting age. Try to work out whether you are left wing, right wing or somewhere in between. See the back of this book for some great organizations that are ace in engaging us normal folk when it comes to politics. Knowing what your choices are is empowering and helpful when it comes to casting your vote, which, by the way, is one of the most important things you will EVER do in your adult life. PLEASE VOTE. We all have the right: people fought for that, so use it. According to recent electoral reform statistics, one in four eighteen to twenty-one-year-olds had not registered to vote. This is not good! Particularly when you consider that in the 1960s over seventy per cent of eighteen to twenty-four-year-olds voted. Now, I'm FULLY aware that the boring admin effort that seems to be involved in registering might not be your priority over all the other things you've got to get sorted. Just know that if you're not voting, then you are not changing all the things that will affect you, and many others like you, the most: our homes, the environment, health care and money. You can do something about that. Take a bit of time to think about what you want from our political system. A younger voice in this country is what's lacking – so use yours.

227

POLITICS

HOW DOES IT MAKE YOU FEEL?

ANGRY?

Head to page 231 for more on how you can convert anger into activism.

CONFUSED?
But want to do more?

Go to www.bitetheballot.co.uk to learn how you can become an active change-maker.

Head to page 231 for tips from a former MP on how to get into politics.

EMPOWERED?
And would love to know how to get into politics further?

OVER-WHELMED?

Go to www.bitetheballot.co.uk to learn how you can become an active change-maker.

MEH?

No power, so it doesn't concern you. Do you use public transport? Do you watch *EastEnders*? Do you get a doctor or hospital appointment for free? Do you pay tax? If you can answer yes to any of those, then it does concern you. Go to www.bitetheballot.co.uk to learn how you can become an active change-maker.

EXCITED?
And politically engaged? Read on!

Go to www.bitetheballot.co.uk to learn how you can become an active change-maker.

A SIMPLE BREAKDOWN OF POLITICAL TERMS

Anarchism: Anarchists believe that the state and forms of compulsory government are harmful or unnecessary to people's lives.

Communism: Communists believe that the capitalist system is damaging to the interests of the masses, and that workers must unite to overthrow it.

Conservatism: Conservative thinking originates in the belief that traditional institutions and modes of government that have evolved over time function the best, and that political change should be organic and not revolutionary.

Environmentalism: Believes in protecting and improving the condition of the natural environment, including greater regulation of human interaction with it, as well as those aspects of our lives that are environmentally unsustainable and damaging.

229

Feminism: Feminists seek full equality in political, social and economic spheres in order to redress the balance in a society and political system that is considered to be patriarchal (run by men!).

Left-wing politics: Usually progressive in nature, left-wing beliefs look to the future, aim to support those who cannot support themselves, are idealist and believe in equality. People who are left-wing believe in taxation to redistribute opportunity and wealth. Institutions like the NHS and the welfare state (e.g. jobseeker's allowance) are fundamentally left-wing ideas.

Liberalism: Liberals believe in protecting the rights of the individual to ensure their maximum freedom – and that civil liberties and freedoms must be safeguarded and protected by the state.

Right-wing politics: These beliefs value tradition, are about equity, survival of the fittest and economic freedom. Right-wing beliefs espouse that business shouldn't be regulated and that freedom for individuals to succeed is paramount over equality.

Socialism: Socialists are motivated to improve the quality of life for every member of society – and believe in the redistribution of resources (including money) to redress inequalities in a free-market economy.

THE ACTIVIST

I got advice from **Jo Swinson**, former Lib Dem MP and government minister and author of *Equal Power*, on how to get involved with changing things that affect you, and those around you:

Voting is important, but there's much more to politics, and lots that you can do even before you're old enough to vote. You can **raise issues with the people elected to represent you** - enter your postcode at **www.theyworkforyou.com** and you'll get the full list of who they are. Email them about the issues you care about or, even better, check when they are holding an 'advice surgery' and go along – this is where you can chat to them face to face, often in a local library or town hall. And campaign to build support for the issues you care about - any UK citizen can **start a petition to parliament.**

Political parties bring together people who share similar ideas about what needs to change. **Joining a party** is a great way to learn about campaigning, and by working with other people your efforts are more likely to make a difference. You can find out about what parties believe on their websites and social media accounts, and by watching programmes like BBC *Question Time*. You don't need to agree one hundred per cent with everything a party says to join, and it's usually only a few pounds for young people, so choose the one that is closest to your views and go for it! And **you're never too young** . . . I was elected as an MP at twenty-five, and in 2015 Mhairi Black was elected as an MP at the age of twenty.

TALKING POLITICS

I asked Josie Long, comedian and co-founder of charity Arts Emergency (whose aim is to ensure the doors of the university are kept open for those most able to benefit from but least able to pay for education) why she thinks it's important to be politicized, and how popular culture and the arts have a definite role to play in humanizing politics.

GC: Why do you think that a lot of people just shy away from politics altogether?

JL: It's definitely easier to not care about it . . . to be complacent. I also think if you're explicitly political, if you pick a side in anything, especially if you come out as anti the status quo a little bit, you're making a real choice in some ways to have people disagree with you and judge you. That can negatively impact your life. I definitely think I've probably lost work because of it, or had arguments with people because of it. But to care about politics is to just care: care about the most wonderful parts of life — and because you think everyone deserves wonderful things. So you care from a position of real joy and love. But sometimes it's easier to think, 'Ya know what — I don't want to have a go at my nice parents who voted in a way I wouldn't.' Or, 'Not everyone who disagrees with me is bad'. . . blah blah blah. So then you can reduce how vocal you are on certain things.

GC: I think that politics affects our emotional well-being — what do you think?

JL: It's interesting, politics, because some people do not have the luxury of choosing whether or not they're involved. If you get kicked out of your council home, it's not a choice. There are so many things like that where it will affect you and hurt you — it comes into your life, and then you have to deal with it. I totally agree with you that the wider sphere of politics impacts on all people . . . Look at climate change — 'Why are the seasons [going] wrong?' Every five minutes you have a conversation with someone where you go, 'This summer's been really weird.' On a deep-rooted level, it's all connected to our political system.

GC: But then when you turn on the telly and you try to understand the news . . . I feel like it's so unrelatable that it's hard to know what to do, and can often render you pretty helpless.

JL: The way the modern world operates — especially with politics — is it convinces you that you're stupid and you know nothing, and it's not for you . . . It's very easy to feel like there's this amorphous mass, and you couldn't possibly do anything. On a local level, a lot of things that used to be participatory community political things have gone. People have to find their communities online or in a more global sense. It's more and more sprawling, so it's harder. The good thing about it is it's a really easy thing to find again. If you scratch the surface in this country, there's people getting on with stuff that you'll be in awe of everywhere, and they need you more than ever. There's volunteer groups, there's community groups, there's activist groups, there's arts groups, there's everything. There's really good groups like Citizens UK, which is the home of community organizing in the UK.

GC: **How important is art when it comes to politics?**

JL: Incredibly so. Think about creativity and critical thought. So, critical thought is obviously the ability to question and the ability to examine; and creativity is the ability to imagine and think up new things and make them. That is how to understand society better, and to be useful to society: understanding what's going on, addressing problems and solving them. I think creativity's massively important for politics. On a very basic level, it lets you imagine something better . . . It's good to know what direction you're pointing in. There's no one that doesn't deserve to be looked after in our society, and there's no one in our society that doesn't deserve to be a fully fledged citizen — even if they're unemployed — everywhere in this country should be habitable.

GC: **What do you do if you don't agree with your best friend or your parents when it comes to politics? How the hell are you supposed to still get on?**

JL: Try to be generous. When it comes down to it, try to put your view across. I think it's very important to learn about how people derail you in arguments, because people love to play devil's advocate — they try to provoke you — and what's quite nice is that you are not necessarily obliged to defend yourself all the time. If you believe things politically, you don't always have to be explaining why. You can just say, 'I have a right to my opinion.'

233

MELTING POT OF
MAD

We live in unbelievably unsettling times. The world over, the unpredictability of how people vote and the actions of others makes me wonder whether the world has lost sight of human kindness. It makes me feel mashed up and tangled inside, raging mad and sad in the pit of my stomach.

I felt saddened and maddened when I heard that a group of young black men in a workshop (held by my performance-artist friend Bryony Kimmings) said that they felt powerless in our political system. I still feel mad from the day that I visited the place where suffragette Emily Wilding Davison (mentioned earlier in the 'Politics' section) was trampled to death by the King's horse in 1913, whilst fighting for votes for women.

I am mad about what I learned when I made a documentary for BBC3 in 2011 about the riots that had set alight some of the UK's major cities the summer before. I am mad and sad for lives ruined, for all those affected in a spiralling mess that largely came from opportunism, materialism and social media rampancy, and an underlying exasperation towards the system. I am mad for the families of those killed in the many acts of terrorism around the world, sickeningly too many to mention. I am sad and mad that the blazing magic-bearers David Bowie and Prince died in 2016. It is impossible not to want to cry every time I am informed of more tragic world news.

. . . And yet the beat goes on. We are a generation more connected and enabled by technology. We will live longer than generations before us. We need to work out what we can do. How can we turn our sadness into action? How can we learn to protest peacefully, educate ourselves so we don't feel so politically powerless and create positive change? Every time I hear of injustice or tragedy – every time I see another repulsive, attention-seeking opportunist shouting and spouting rage and hatred online – it makes me want to stomp out the shoot of despair it creates inside me, and instead plant a seed of warmth and love, which can grow and spread joy in its place.

One thing I do know is that no one should ever, EVER combat violence with violence. The sweetest revenge of all is LOVE. Love is the most powerful thing on this planet. Perhaps we need to turn off regular newsfeeds on our devices and only delve into news about the world's disasters and sadness when we feel like we are ready to do so. I feel there is a balance to be struck between staying informed and protecting our own mental health.

We must remember it is not all doom and gloom, even when we are at our most fearful. Being mindful of the sheer number of joy-filled happenings that occur on this planet can help us combat even the most horrific news. Seek that joy, that goodness, out. A sunset will always be beautiful; an embrace will always bring warmth and safety. Plus there are some phenomenal people in the world doing phenomenal things for good. Be one of them.

A checklist for living in this political world

- ☐ It is OK to cry. It is OK to be angry. But learn to channel this into something spectacular.
- ☐ Discuss, ask questions and educate yourself.
- ☐ Use your right to vote.
- ☐ As long as the world still exists, there will always be hope. Go find it.
- ☐ Remember how important you are – you are great . .

you – yes YOU – can change the world.

EXPERIENCE

We each experience life uniquely. The most important thing is to find our own voice, and learn how to use it – this is invaluable, regardless of political stance. To feel rooted like a tree in your loves, your dislikes and your wants for your world is a way of affirming your place in it. I asked writer Frances Acquaah, from South London, to open up and write about her world and experiences. (You can read more from Frances on pages 52–4 in 'Your Heart'.)

#NOFILTER
by Frances Acquaah

I pretty much had my whole life planned out growing up — putting age stamps on future life milestones. By twenty-eight I was going to own my dream house before being swept off my feet by Prince Charming. After having children (including at least one set of twins), we would build our empire, travel the world and retire early.

Needless to say, life has happened, and any hope of the above coming true is as mythical as the fairy-tale ending I had imagined. At least not any time soon. I do still possess hope, though.

Though it does feel like we are all pretty much doomed on the dream-house front . . . especially if you live in a city.

A report by Aviva predicts that by 2025 a third of young adults will have to move back into their childhood bedroom.

At the end of the day, none of the main parties are doing anything in the interest of young people. None of them are fighting our corner; they are too busy throwing shade at each other in parliament, and only care to give us a second thought when it's campaign time. That's how it seems, anyway.

I was the first person from my immediate family to go to university. I didn't really see it as an achievement at the time, because my Sixth Form made it seem like it was the next natural step — there was no other option. Now I am waist deep in thousands of pounds of debt, and although I made some lifelong friends it is far from worth it.

Like many, when I left university I felt a sense of entitlement and pride; I thought I was too good for retail, and I definitely wasn't going to sign on. Getting a degree meant access to better, higher-paid jobs — so I had been told. It was a very humbling experience when I had to return back to the shop floor, to say the least. Somehow, six months later, I managed to land myself a job in a role that was actually relevant to my degree. Luckily, I've been working in the media industry ever since.

In this financial climate, not everyone has been as fortunate as myself, and many graduates have had to put their dream career on hold in order to survive, working in admin, recruitment agencies or call centres — just some of the more popular roles graduates tend to take on so they can escape retail.

When I was working as an editor of a youth magazine, some of the younger contributors taught me some of the unwritten rules for Instagram. The one that stuck and shocked me the most was the 'one-like-per-minute rule'. Apparently, once you have uploaded a picture, if you don't get at least one like per minute, it means your picture isn't going to 'perform well' — so many young people will just delete it out of embarrassment.

This is their reality; this is where we are.

I see myself as a bit of a piggy in the middle. I'm in a unique position where the internet is second nature, but still I would give it up in a heartbeat if it was a choice between that and natural daylight.

Unfortunately, many of us place our value on how many 'likes' we get and how many people are following us across our social media. So many young people (and adults) are chasing ideals of beauty that only exist after multiple filters have been applied, and we are allowing brands to capitalize every day on insecurities we didn't even know we had.

There are people doing gymnastics so the lens can capture their red-bottom shoes all for the validation of people they have never met! And I'm not saying it's bad to have expensive things, but you can't say you don't care what people think of you on one hand, but then say you can't wear an outfit because you've previously posted it on social media.

Oh, and let's not forget hashtag [insert] goals — from someone else's body, to their relationships, to what they had for breakfast. It's exhausting.

We've barely touched the surface with regards to research on the links between social media and mental health. Like you'll never know how my fourteen-year-old cousin laughed in my face when he saw my Snapchat score — I didn't realize it was a competition. You'll only be aware of the true extent of it all if you are on the ground.

In order to overcome FOMO, we can't be constantly glued to our phones. It's so important to use everything in balance. Let your social media be an extension of your truth, and learn to love what you see when you look at yourself without the filters.

The decisions you make about your life will affect you in the long run, no one else. Take in every moment in the present and enjoy it; it's not necessary to Snapchat it all the time.

GENERATION DIY

The government's lack of concern for young people means that we have had no option but to create our own opportunities.

One good thing that has risen from our lack of prospects is the number of start-ups driven by young people. A study by Hays revealed that the majority of Generation Y viewed the idea of becoming an entrepreneur attractive, with sixty-one per cent either having their own business or interested in running one in the future.

Initially dubbed a 'lazy generation', we have proven that we are in fact the complete opposite: ambitious, business savvy and innovative — they should consider renaming us 'Generation DIY'.

239

OUR NATURAL WORLD

Our environment sometimes seems a little poorly, doesn't it? You can feel it in the air when we experience erratic weather – wetter, windier winters . . . drier, more sweltering summers. And when we learn of natural disasters around the world, like the fierce hurricanes that savage towns and ravage people's lives, our hearts ache at our sense of powerlessness.

BUT we all have the potential to help. When thinking about our environment, is it important to know that if we collectively become more conscious of what we can do to protect it then it could be possible to halt a lot of environmental damage, just by introducing small changes into our day-to-day lives.

But we need to do it TOGETHER. Ignite passion for our planet!

240

EIGHT SIMPLE WAYS TO DO YOUR BIT

1 Reduce. Reuse. Recycle. If you don't recycle your rubbish, then WHY don't you? If you live with your parents or in a shared house that hasn't got into recycling, then you be the ONE that starts, and get everyone else to do it too.

2 Take it a step further and start a compost heap (compost is decayed organic material used as fertilizer to grow plants). Most local councils can provide you with a composting bin to get you on your merry green serene way.

3 When you have a special event that you are buying an outfit for, think about ethical and eco-friendly clothing. Research the brands that make beautiful clothes without exploiting people or the environment, and you can get yourself an ethically sound outfit. Or the next time you are buying a new pair of shoes, think about where you get them from. Beyond Skin, for example, make bangingly brilliant vegan faux-leather shoes.

4 Go for a spree in your local charity shop (I have honestly found some of my greatest purchases in charity shops – including a full tweed suit, a fluorescent-yellow ski jacket and a Hollywood-worthy faux-fur grizzly-bear-brown coat).*

5 Get a washing line if you don't have one already; tumble dryers guzzle energy at a monstrous rate.

6 Grow your own vegetables. Even if you don't have a garden, you can invest in a vegetable growbag. They are wicked for balconies, patios and small front gardens. The joy of growing is too humungous to ignore. (Head to page 246 for more on plants.)

7 Get a beehive!! (More on this on pages 242–4.)

8 Sign up to the Greenpeace newsletter to stay informed on the globe, its challenges and how we can help.

*If you successfully buy a brilliant outfit from a charity shop that you adore, please take a snap and share it, tagging me @gemagain, and announcing that you're #TeamOpen. I wanna see all the immense charity-shop bargains!

NATURAL HOBBIES

BELIEVE IT OR NOT, not *everything* fun is to be found online. Did you know there are so many things we can do that don't cost much money and don't involve a keyboard or a screen . . . just our natural resources and the wonderful world around us?

Bees do it better.

Bees – what beguiling and fascinating creatures they are, not only the inspiration for the colour scheme of *Open*, being yellow and black, but genuinely vital to our environment too.

I interviewed Becca, a fifteen-year-old beekeeper, to find out more about this essential and illuminating badass hobby.

Local Honey

GC: I believe that we as humans could learn from bee life. Would you agree?

B: Yeah, bees are what people describe as a super-organism: every bee in the hive has a job. One thing I find very interesting about bees is that when they sting you they will die — but they're not doing it because they feel frightened; they do it because they feel their colony is endangered. They're not selfish at all, which I really find quite cool. Another interesting fact is that the majority of the bees in the hive are girl bees. It's a peculiar fact, but the boy bees are only there to mate with a new queen . . . this is their only reason to be. In the winter, the girl bees kick them out of the hive. The girl bees are the more important ones.

GC: How has beekeeping changed your life?

B: The best thing that beekeeping's done for me is created loads of opportunities. I've gone across Europe with bees, and I've talked to other people from all over the world, where we have different backgrounds but such a common interest — beekeeping. It's a nice thing to bond over.

GC: People out there might think, 'Oh, I live somewhere where I just couldn't have a hive,' or, 'This just isn't for me.' Are there ways of making it work in a city?

B: You don't really have to have a large amount of land: I know of people that keep bees on roofs of buildings. It's really quite easy to keep them in most areas.

GC: How does beekeeping enhance your life?

B: I personally think it's great and everybody should learn about it, because it makes you look at the world from a different point of view. You suddenly start to think, 'Well, without bees we wouldn't have this, or we wouldn't have that.' It's a constant reminder that they're such an important part of our world.

243

GC: Have you been stung before?

B: Yep. Normally I try not to get stung because it hurts, but it does occasionally happen.

GC: I went to Ethiopia in East Africa with Oxfam, and I met with beekeepers there living in tiny villages, who were changing the face of their communities by gaining an income from making and then selling honey. The fact that the women would do it from home, bring up families and beekeep was perfect for their lifestyles. Would you be interested in travelling around the world and finding out more about beekeeping?

B: Definitely. There is an organization called Bees Abroad, and they go to developing countries. I was speaking to somebody the other day, and they said that there was girl who paid for her education all the way up to university through keeping bees.

GC: It's a really beautiful way of connecting to others and our natural world.

B: Yeah. Me, my sister and my dad beekeep together, and my mum helps bottle all the honey — it is a real family thing. We also take our bees to do demonstrations and chat to the public.

GC: So for those that don't know, how does it improve the world to look after bees?

B: Without beekeepers, honeybees wouldn't be able to survive in this country because there are certain diseases and pests which will kill them off. So what we're doing is we're helping them survive, which helps pollinate plants, giving us fruits and flowers and a happier, healthier environment.

GC: And a constant supply of honey. We can't dismiss THAT — that is so good!

B: Quite a lot of my friends keep saying, 'Becca, can I have a jar of honey?' It is really nice, because it's a standalone thing, which only I do . . . It's really interesting, and it makes me different from everybody else. I like that in a way. I like being different.

245

PLANTS

Pssssssssssssssssssttttttt. It's fun to go potty with planting. It makes your insides smile to nurture a living thing. It automatically roots you to nature. Whether it's a miniature cactus or a glorious, giant *Oxalis triangularis* – aka the butterfly plant . . . aka purple shamrocks – fill your house and surround yourself with them. There are thousands of videos on YouTube giving advice on how to look after specific plants.

With so much of our time spent in front of computer screens for work, games and social media, not to mention hours spent watching television, it's more vital than ever that we find ways to switch off. By far the best antidote to the demands of our increasingly busy work and school schedules, is to get outdoors and enjoy the beauty of nature. Growing your own plants, be they roses in the garden, cheerful daisies and snapdragons to cut and put in a vase, or harvesting home-grown crops of fresh fruit, veg and herbs, can be great fun. Gardening will also help keep you fit and be hugely rewarding when everything blooms. I absolutely guarantee that once you've tried it you'll be hooked! Happy gardening!

Rachel de Thame

TREES

Just as bees are super important for our natural environment, so are trees. Trees are the most dynamic natural resource we have. Not only do they look like glorious, wise old creatures – they also clean the air we breathe by absorbing pollutants and generating oxygen. Those lovely special trees, they create habitats for wildlife, helping species to survive and thrive. They provide protection from weather extremes and prevent surface water flooding. They transform our landscapes. They are a part of our history and national identity. They are good for our health – research has found that people who live in greener areas experience lower levels of mental distress and have a better quality of life. What is not to LOVE about trees?

We can do our bit to keep our trees growing and thriving. We need to stand up for them as they are under constant threat from redevelopment. Find out what is happening to large areas of tree-filled green around where you live. If there are redevelopment plans for any of them, then write to your local council and your MP (more on how you can do this on page 231). Tell your friends to do the same. Volunteer for the Woodland Trust, who are dedicated to the protection of our native trees and woodlands. Get involved! Now go and give a tree a hug, at the risk of sounding insane I have tried this a few times and it feels bizarrely joyous.

The ability to communicate is liberating and cool. To load up with the good words, learn them – let them wrap around you and protect you. Fill your heart and mind with the tools of talking. Arm yourself with your beautiful language. Words empower you. Words make life more interesting and beautiful too. A good vocabulary is enriching – a brilliant tool for creativity.

Play the word puzzle below, and see which words you can identify with.

```
        S W W C               H S W Q
      F V W B J G            O D E O M M
    R A I E X D I Q      B G M V W K P I
  N E N N D A I V I A G E F T I D X P B X
Z Y H T Z R C F K F F N J C V S V N O Y N T
J V N T A U A I F A J I I D A C S J M L K P N Y
X D E O S K G M E B D S R T I A E G U E A Q A R
I O W R T W E I R D O G E N D L R N G N C X I D
U M P F I E S C E O D M E B I T G L T O S X L I
X Y F R C F D P N B Y Y N V O E O L J R K O L C
C Z L Z A S A K T Q O E O D S R R T W C I J I X
  A E P L E W A M U O M I D Y N P C E A F C R
  E T V Y A S H S I E K P J N A P N G V C X B
    S N I X C T R R M K W S C T H I A A N E
    N M T F I S K P N M J R I T T Z N V
      T Q A X D Y X V F J A V U S H T
      G Z V U A U C L I T E V I R
      Z K O M R U A A I G Z D
      E Q N W J H I C A U
      Y X N S V V L M
        G C I B G Y
        M N O Y
        X Q
```

ALTERNATIVE	**DISTINCT**	**IDIOSYNCRATIC**	**PROGRESSIVE**
AVANT	**ECCENTRIC**	**INNOVATIVE**	**QUIRKY**
BRILLIANT	**FANTASTICAL**	**OTHER**	**RADICAL**
DIFFERENT	**GARDE**	**PIONEERING**	

Alternative: 1) one or more things available as another possibility or choice and 2) relating to activities that depart from or challenge traditional norms

Avant garde: original or innovative (especially with reference to popular music)

Brilliant: 1) very bright light or colour and 2) exceptionally clever or talented

Different: 1) not the same as another or each other, unlike in nature, form or quality and 2) distinct, separate

Distinct: 1) recognizably different in nature from something else of similar type and 2) readily distinguishable by the senses

Eccentric: 1) unconventional and slightly strange person and 2) not placed centrally, or not having its axis or other part placed centrally

Fantastical: 1) conceived or appearing as conceived by an unrestrained imagination and 2) odd, bizarre, grotesque

Idiosyncratic: relating to idiosyncracy – peculiar or individual

Innovative: 1) relating to a product, idea, etc., one featuring new methods and 2) advanced and original

Other: 1) used to refer to a person or thing that is different or distinct from one already mentioned and 2) further, additional

Pioneering: involving new ideas or methods

Progressive: 1) happening or developing gradually or in stages and 2) of a person or idea, favouring social reform

Quirky: having or characterized by peculiar or unexpected traits or aspects

Radical: 1) (especially of change or action) relating to or affecting the fundamental nature of something and 2) characterized by departure from tradition, innovative or progressive

THE INTERNET

The other world we increasingly inhabit is the worldwide web. The internet is a good place to find your tribe, your community and people with similar ideals – through platforms, blogs and online discussion forums. It's great for catching up with friends and family members who live around the world. It's hilarious for goats that sound as if they are talking! It's bad for browsing or stalking – how much time is spent looking at trousers or our ex's new partner? It's horrific for the amount of lies and death and doom it fills your brain with. It's toxic, with evil people trying to get you to spend money to talk to them. It's ugly when people are mean. It's dangerously obsessive.

There are as many bits to the internet world as there are to the real one. Living in TWO WORLDS is EXHAUSTING! In order not to let it 'cage us' we should load ourselves with the knowledge of its potential and face up to how it can affect us, for better or worse. This involves embracing the fantastic side of tech innovation, but also it means treating the internet the same way as we would anything that is bad for our health or that we could get addicted to – RESPONSIBLY. ALSO acquaint yourself with the power of the plug. The plug is as powerful as a lightsaber against negativity, and YOU have the power to switch the internet off, whenever you want. That 'off' button is your friend and, thankfully, there's loads of other fun things to do in life.

SIX DIZZYING INTERNET FACTS

1 In China there are treatment camps for internet addicts. Two hundred million internet users in China are between the ages of fifteen and thirty-five, and that demographic is seen as the most 'likely' to lose self-control. Tao Ran, director of the country's first internet-addiction treatment clinic in Beijing, said that forty per cent of those addicted to the internet suffer from attention deficit hyperactivity disorder, also known as ADHD.

2 According to common folklore, the first emoticon was created by a bloke called Kevin MacKenzie in 1979 and looked like . . . drum roll, pleeeeease . . . this: -)

3 It is estimated that eighty per cent of all images on the internet are of naked women.

4 For a period in 2013, the first autofill that would pop up if you typed 'Is it legal to' was 'own a sloth?'. Yep, 'Is it legal to own a sloth?' At the time of writing this book, the first thing that comes up is, 'Is it legal to marry your cousin?' Ermmm . . .

5 A very brainy physicist called Russell Seitz has worked out that the ENTIRE internet weighs approximately as much as one single strawberry.

6 Every sixty seconds over seventy-two hours of YouTube content is uploaded. That's too much to keep on top of, I reckon.

251

THE INTERNET
(THE WORLDWIDE WEB)

THE GOOD STUFF

There are SO MANY benefits to using the internet. Things like connectivity – the amount of people you can stay in touch with now; globalization; **self-education** – *click*, *click*, *click*. So much amazing information is readily there for us. Finding like-minded others is awesome – your scene, your community. And one of the greatest things the internet does is facilitate **self-exploration** – you can play with your identity online in a way that you can't play with it offline.

So the internet is an amazingly good thing in so many ways. From finding long-lost friends, to researching for your studies, to having an amazing fun-filled chat with your best mate who lives far away. Skype, FaceTime, they keep us close when we can't physically be with someone. The likes of Instagram can bring out the creativity in us and share it. It can make you feel less alone. It can make you smile. So far so good.

THE STUFF THAT CAN HURT US

With the help of Dr Alison Attrill-Smith, senior lecturer in Cyber Psychology at the University of Wolverhampton, who heads up one of the biggest cyber psychology research groups in the UK, we came up with this comprehensive guide of what we need to be aware of, wary of and responsible for when it comes to the internet.

BOUNDARIES

A boundary is the line marking the limits of an area, and boundaries are usually in place for a good reason. Research proves that the **boundaries of internet use** are becoming very flexible when it comes to how younger people behave online. One of the obvious examples is revenge porn, which many people access and use without realizing it is wrong.

Revenge porn is the sharing of private sexual materials, either photos or videos, of another person without their consent and with the purpose of causing embarrassment or distress.

Revenge porn is a new offence, recognized by UK law, that applies both online and offline and to images which are shared electronically or in a more traditional way, so it includes the uploading of images on the internet, sharing by text or email, or showing someone a physical or electronic image.

If you are worried about anything regarding this subject, head to www.revengepornhelpline.org.uk

YOUR DIGITAL FOOTPRINT

People think they're anonymous online. They are not. In the early stages of internet communication, people *were* anonymous, but that's no longer the case. It's so easy to find someone's true identity – their digital footprint – online. It's important to remember this before you post anything. Ask yourself, *'Would I say this in the real world? Would I want my family to see this?'* Even if you delete something quickly, the thing about online posts is that they never really go away. Within seconds, someone may have screen-grabbed it, or may at least remember it. Your actions can have huge consequences online.

Technology records things, IP addresses, etc. You are never anonymous online nowadays. So just think about what you're putting online. The danger is sharing information across a lot of different sites. Everywhere you share data it's recorded; it can be connected to you. Google yourself. Everyone should Google themselves every now and then to see what is out there about them.

Think about WHAT you're sharing. Why would you write, 'I'm by the pool wherever,' to let the world know that your home's empty. So there's that side of it as well. Just give it up, just go away and enjoy, and connect to life again without the digital technology. Believe it or not, that is possible, and it is usually more satisfying.

ACCEPTABLE BEHAVIOUR

Our thresholds of acceptability are getting higher and higher. We have access to so much that is potentally disturbing and is unregulated. Just because there is lots of nudity out there, doesn't mean we need to join in. If someone asks you to send them a nude or sexy picture of yourself, or you feel the urge to for fun, think twice about how this picture could come back to haunt you. Do you really want your privacy invaded like that? It may not matter much to you right now, but what about in ten years' time? Think about it.

SEARCHING FOR VALIDATION AND BELONGING

We all have this notion that we need to belong; we need to feel like we're wanted, that we fit in to the human race somehow, somewhere. If people are seeking that online, it's vital to be aware of the potential consequences. It may be that you don't get what you're looking for or you get more than you bargained for: it's very easy to be ignored or ridiculed online and that can have a huge impact on self-esteem. Be aware of the consequences of how you behave with others online too. Posting negative or unkind comments just to be funny can potentially hurt others as much as if you said it to their face. If you can't say anything nice then don't say anything at all.

255

Our obsessive 'like culture' is all about validation. It's easy to feel that if you get ten likes, that's ten affirmations and you are doing good – you are an acceptable human being. This also means that if you get lots of likes for saying or posting something negative or unkind you might feel that your behaviour is acceptable, when it isn't. Be aware that posting anything just to get likes can lead to self-destructive behaviour and damage others. Importantly, 'likes' online, often from strangers, can never create the happy hormones in the brain that are released from real human interaction.

One thing we can all do with the technology we have access to now is actually edit how we look and so present what we feel are improved (in some cases radically different) versions of our faces and our bodies. Though it can be fun to put an **'add ons' filter** on your images, it can become obsessive, so much so that without realizing it we are rejecting real selves for not being good enough. Think about how sad that is! What you look like in real life counts the most. Look in the mirror, pull fun faces at your real reflection – it's sometimes hard to remember what we look like if we're constantly viewing it through a screen with animated 'Disney character' eyes stuck on over our own.

Online dating can give us a sense of 'limitlessness' when it comes to potential partners, and creates a flippancy when it comes to meeting people. Awareness of both your behaviour and that of others is particularly important here. Be aware of weird behaviour, be cautious and manage your expectations. If you are searching for 'love' rather than 'fun', you need to be extra careful. Though online dating can be a decent and fun way to meet people, it's not the ONLY ANSWER. If you want to try it, you should research which one is the right one for you (there are SO many), you should ALWAYS meet someone in a public space and remember that people can be totally different to who they say they are online. Like I said earlier, the ability to edit words and pictures means people can misrepresent themselves to a ridiculous degree without thinking about what they're doing. An extreme example of this is catfishing.

Catfishing is an online dating phenomenon where one person creates a fake identity to woo another, often using fake pictures and a fake name. Sometimes a lot of time is spent building a relationship via messaging and emails, but lots of it is based on lies. The longer it goes on, the more time and emotion you invest in that person, building up an image of them in your head that you really want to be true. Catfish relationships can go on for a long time, and typically don't result in a meet-up. But if the deceit is uncovered, the fall-out for the person who has been fooled can be very damaging. The catfish themselves isn't always a bad person. A lot of the time their own insecurities, their own low self-esteem, is why they don't want to come clean. This is why it's important that we should all be cautious, take care of ourselves and don't invest in someone you have never met.

DIGITAL DETOX

So, now you know all the pros and cons, it's time to shake up your internet life and possibly take a step back. That feeling of crappiness you have constantly looking at your phone? It might be down to over-use, to your loss of perspective.

Monitor the amount of time you spend online. Ask yourself honestly: *could* you be using some of your **time more productively?**

It can be fun to experiment by logging out of your social media accounts from time to time. Test how long you can survive, note if you feel any different. Another good way of trying this is to switch off notifications on your phone, or by taking off your email on mobile devices. It can help you feel **less frazzled. Read a book, plug in your iPod, go hiking, get your actual camera and go and take some beautiful pictures. Enjoy your Real Life.**

257

IRL VS URL QUIZ, ANYONE?

When you put your phone or device down after a boredom-filling sesh, you realize you've been looking at it for . . .

A Between 0–30 minutes.

B Between 30 minutes to an hour.

C More than an hour.

On holiday you and your phone . . .

A Have a much needed break from each other and it is switched off most of the time.

B Comes everywhere with you, but you only check it a couple of times a day and make a point of not posting too much on social media.

C Are letting all your mates see constantly what amazoid food you are eating, how much you are in love with the sights, your sun-kissed body and perfected holiday pose.

When you are online you are mostly . . .

A On social media talking to your friends and looking at cute dogs.

B Doing a) above and ordering stuff you don't need.

C Doing all of a) and b) above and you sometimes end up down rabbit holes looking at stuff that makes you feel a bit icky.

258

Which statement do you agree with the most on the subject of what's acceptable to share online (even in a private-message capacity)?

A I would never post anything I wouldn't say out loud or would hate my family to see.

B I sometimes regret being a little ranty/over-excited.

C I definitely have shared images, messages or comments I regret.

If someone's written something nasty about you online, do you . . .

A Report them straight away?

B Feel upset, reply to them and then try to forget about it?

C Stew on it for a long time, thinking their nasty words might be true?

How many tabs do you usually have open at one time when on the computer?

A 1–5

B 5–10

C More

Have you noticed how, when you search for something, similar products are advertised for you at a later date, sometimes on different sites?

A Yes, you are aware that cookies store up to create your digital footprint and that advertisers work with this information so they know how to target you.

B You've noticed but you try not think about it too much.

C You had NO idea.

With your best mate you would prefer to . . .

A Go to the cinema.

B Skype – it's easier to fit in.

C You have loads of best mates and most of them you keep in touch with on endless WhatsApp chat.

259

MOSTLY As - You're an IRLer, ella, ella!

You are mainly motivated by things in real life and feel you have a healthy under-standing and grip of how the online world can affect you. You protect yourself and harness your online time and relationships carefully. You mostly live your life in the real world and don't really understand how people take it all so seriously.

MOSTLY Bs - You're the common keyboarder!

You are likely to end up stuck in an online hole for a little longer than you'd like sometimes, but you are keen to brush up on your knowledge of the ever-evolving technology.

Head to **www.bbc.co.uk/webwise** for guides and answers to lots of questions on internet facts and safety.

MOSTLY Cs - You're a cybermaniac!

You are probably spending a little too much time online and sometimes feel a bit down, but don't know why. You act impulsively online and don't always think about what you are putting out there. It's time to try not to always rely on your phone and devices for company. Reconnect with the real world and challenge yourself. Don't have your mobile near when you are eating food with people. Read a book from cover to cover. Spend a whole Sunday with your phone switched off and no access to a computer or connected device. It would also be a good idea to head to the WebWise site suggested above in MOSTLY Bs so that you can get clued up on certain things about being online and, with the basics under your belt, still enjoy surfing the web.

D-I-Y EXPRESSION

Immerse yourself in the good stuff: stuff that makes you happy, that helps you create and celebrate your world the way you want to. One of the ways of doing this is to start your own zine – a collection of stories, ideas, visuals and writing on the types of subjects you are interested in and that you think the world might be lacking.

GAL POWER

gal-dem.com is a creative online magazine comprising the contributions of over seventy women of colour. They wanted people of different shapes, sizes, genders and ethnic backgrounds to engage with the work they are doing.

gal-dem editor Liv has provided *Open* with five tips on how to start a zine.

1 One of the first things we decided on for the magazine was the theme. Deciding on a clear theme made deciding the rest somewhat straightforward. We knew what sort of pieces we wanted and which writers, artists and photographers would be a good fit. In terms of producing a coherent magazine, this was key!

2 The second key point is being clear with the sort of pieces you want to publish. We put out an open call for submissions, but we didn't accept every single idea. It can be really tricky deciding what content to publish, but it largely came down to us not wanting to reproduce similar pieces and maintain our chatty gal-dem tone. There will always be pieces which simply don't fit! I know when I first started editing I hated having these conversations – but there are definitely ways to be diplomatic.

3 Reaching out to people whose work you *fan-girl* over. Many of the photographers and writers involved in this print were people whose work I loved and hadn't worked with before. Our budget was non-existent (and print is very expensive!), so we had to reach out to people and be open and honest about what it was we could offer, but mainly getting them on board with the ethos behind gal-dem. If you are backing a worthy cause, the chances are people will rally behind you if they can.

4 You will always find the odd mistake in print, particularly if it's your first one. But the best way to minimize risk is to have a rigorous team of editors and sub-editors. All pieces should be looked at a minimum of twice. It's definitely best not to leave this until the eleventh hour, when you are tired and have been staring at the same pages for hours. Get different people to check different pieces as they will always find something you may miss.

5 Print is expensive and there will always be hidden costs. So the final tip would have to be always overestimate how much things will cost, and set up things like pre-orders beforehand. Fortunately I had friends and family who offered to lend me money without asking, but we still ended up going over budget. We ordered as many copies as we could to keep our costs down and it definitely paid off. People are willing to pay for something substantial – they generally want something which they can pop on their coffee table and flick through at their own leisure.

Head to www.gal-dem.com for more.

THAT'S WHAT SHE SAID

There are so many exciting grassroots movements out there, one of them being *thatswhatss*, an amazing photography and expression platform for girls. I spoke to **Izzy Whiteley** from That's What She Said – thatswhatss – about what drives her.

GC: **What is thatswhatss, exactly?**

I: That's What She Said is a photography-based project that aims to be the middleman between young girls and non-binary teens and society. We go around the UK, working on creative projects, with the aim of creating an open line of communication between these young people and society. It is ultimately about giving them a voice - away from the judgement of peers, teachers and parents. The topics are about everything relating to girlhood.

I really want to give girls and non-binary teens a platform to voice their opinions. I want to encourage them to question society and make a project that will force the issue, because we are bringing up a generation of girls that don't believe in themselves and, more importantly, are silenced. Many of them don't even know they have opinions until you ask them a certain question and it all comes pouring out.

We also have a 'She Said' section for submissions, which can be anything from art, essays, random thoughts and poems, to videos and music. From these submissions I find creative ways to write their quotes and share them on Instagram. All we want is to capture the beauty of reality,

264

and give these teens space and safety to talk about issues that they often feel people don't care about or don't think are important. It is giving the power back to people and, hopefully, encouraging them to fight for change.

GC: Why did you feel the need to create it?

I: When I was a young girl, I never really questioned why I felt so bad. I felt ugly, fat, inadequate - not good enough for society and men. From what I read in magazines and in the media and through talking to friends, I felt that it was normal to be a girl and feel bad. Everything around me was telling me that I was flawed and that I needed to be better. We expect girls to feel ugly, cry all the time, be weak and take dangerous measures to change their appearance because 'it's just what girls do'. We did not come out of the vagina hating our thighs and sexualizing ourselves. This is what we have been taught.

When creating thatswhatss I felt like we never hear real experiences — just facts, figures and percentages. Though data collection is sometimes the only way, there is so much more info and things to learn from each teen's voice — and, more importantly, they are the ones that can tell us what to change. I wanted to listen to their experiences, pain, worries, fears, find out what they need, and take it to where it needs to go.

I realized quickly that teens need to be educated about this idea of conditioning and the blame that is put on us surrounding 'choice'. Choice is not simply black and

265

white — it is shades of grey, which represent the pressures that make us choose to do, or not do, something. Some of these choices we are aware of, and some we aren't. All these particular choices such as dieting, changing our appearance, sexualization, etc. are being made in a society where women are still not economically, politically or socially equal. From the day a girl is born, she is bombarded with more and more signs that her worth is in her looks. Feminism is just much more complicated now as the issues aren't so black and white; many issues are subtle and harder to understand. There can be this ugly 'uncool' stigma around feminism, which makes teens not want to be part of it — thatswhatss represents the individual's voice and that's why I chose to start it.

It takes a lot of confidence and self-assurance to be an activist — thatswhatss is a space where young girls and non-binary teens can talk about these issues without having to fight against everyone. There are so many extremes of feminism, which when you are just starting out can be really intimidating. I wanted to give teens a way to just dip their foot in and start understanding the injustice.

GC: Do you have any tips for those out there who want to create something similar?

I: Research the hell out of it. See what's out there. See how your idea is different. It's good when it comes from your own experiences, because the passion always comes through. Make sure you have support and people who believe in you, who can help you along the way. You don't have to have everything figured out before you start; you can change and grow as you go along. Contact and reach out to everyone and anyone, but don't be disheartened when people don't reply, even after the fifth email. I have contacted and chased so, so much press. Rejection can be hard to deal with, but people are so busy, and you are often asking for help without offering anything. Don't take it personally.

Ask advice and learn from people. I have had so many meetings with people that I thought would be 'the big break', and they have turned into nothing — which is OK, because you keep learning, but it can be a bit annoying. Make sure it is something you really enjoy, because you will be spending a lot of your free time on it.

Head to www.thatswhatss.com
for more info.
Instagram @thatswhatss

267

VOLUNTEERING

Is something so fabulous to do!

Fabulous for your mind, fabulous for skill building, fabulous for the organization you offer your time to, fabulous for your community. Volunteering can take up as little or as much of your life as you want it to. There are an abundance of schemes offering the opportunity to get involved in a way that suits you.

For example, you could go on the Age UK website, sign up and before you know it you could end up making a new friend in someone older and wiser who can offer you a different perspective on life. Volunteering to work in Oxfam shops would be a fantastic way to gain shop-floor skills and meet new people. Plus specialist organizations can even arrange volunteering opportunities for you abroad.

Head to the back of this book for a list of organizations looking for volunteers.

THE SCARY WORLD

Your world is often what you make it . . . but some people feel like they have had that choice taken away from them, and like they want to run away. Do you ever feel like that? Are you worried about someone who does?

269

Running away can mean putting yourself in a very unsafe situation – and will change the lives of those you are running away from too. It's an extremely serious thing to do. Both parties need to know that there is help out there.

I spoke to the amazing fire-flame that is Karen Robinson from Missing People about the incredible organization. She tells us:

Running away is not always necessarily a deliberate thing. A lot of people find themselves in a situation where they need to get out and they go – they don't make a decision necessarily to vanish from their life, but once they're gone it's sometimes very hard to come back.

A lot of missing adults who've been found safe and well and who've returned talk about a series of small decisions, find it gets harder and harder to contact whatever 'home' is. So they end up being missing because they might think to themselves, 'Well, how do I explain? If I didn't go home tonight, how would I explain to my boyfriend tomorrow why I didn't go home tonight?' So then it becomes, 'Well, I'll stay away another night.' And then, 'How do I explain why I was away for two nights? By that time, my whole family will know. How am I going to explain to my family what's going on in my head?'

So it's more complicated than you see in films. We know that around 250,000 people a year will go missing, and two-thirds of those are under eighteen – they're children – but that's just the ones that we know about.

If you are a missing person, I think the most important thing is to get help from someone you trust. You might not want to re-approach your life, and that's completely OK. It's OK not to want to be in touch with the people who are missing you. It's perfectly OK; it's not a crime. The charity Missing People is not going to judge you for that and we are here twenty-four hours a day, confidentially and for free. Anyone can call or text us on the number 116000 day or night and we will listen and help. We will never judge you.

So we would encourage people to contact us if they want some completely anonymous, confidential, neutral support, or a space to think through their options. We will help the person decide what they want, what to do next and help them be connected to a safe place or adult. Sometimes we make three-way calls to social workers and police, or we help people access help from a local hostel so they can have a warm bed for the night. We never rush people. It can take time to work out how you feel and decide what you want and that's OK.

We can pass a message home if someone wants to send their family or carers a message if they aren't ready to speak to them yet. It's sometimes the first step. Through our helpline, we speak to tens of thousands of people every year who do want to let their loved ones know that they're OK, but aren't ready to go back. We'll pass messages between them — and/or pass a message home . . . until they're ready to be in touch. There are so many emotions in there, but we can be a bit of a bridge between the two.

If the situation you are running from is unsafe, you don't have to go back. You don't have to love where you are living, and you don't have to love someone just because they're your blood relative. It's OK to be angry with your relatives or your carers (if you're living in care). We can reconnect people via three-way calls as well — not necessarily with their loved ones; quite often it will be with the police, or a social worker, or a teacher — somebody who is a safe adult.

Trust your gut — if you're worried about someone, it's probably for a good reason. If you can't find them and it's out of the ordinary and you're concerned, ring the police and report them missing. The police will ask you lots of questions and decide if and how they can help. Try to reach the person yourself, contact other people they hang out with and try to work out what's going on. Then contact us at the charity Missing People by calling or texting 116000. We can help you clear your head a bit, and go, 'Right, have you thought of this? Are there other children in the house?' If it's a missing child, people literally go into shock, panic, trauma mode. We are here to help you, guide you and support you at what will be one of the most frightening moments of your life.

Most missing people will be found very quickly, and they'll be found safe and well. More than ninety per cent of people will be found within twenty-four hours. A tiny fraction of people who go missing will stay missing for a long period of time, and some of them stay missing for years or even decades. Missing People will be with that family throughout, and hold their hand through it all.

Go to **www.missingpeople.org.uk** for more information on this brilliant charity and how it can help.

PREJUDICE

Noun: *a preconceived optinion that is not based on reason or actual experience*

HATE IS A WASTE – RACISM A DISGRACE

Us humans have complicated and active brains pulling us in many directions. We are full of contradictions; at times we cavort like a rhino on champagne, but then – within the blink of an eye – revert to a terrified mouse. Our morality is easily twisted, our hopes and dreams yanked in one direction and then the other as we bumble through life, the temptations of greed, and sour grapes of envy and discontent sometimes blurring our once-clear vision.

Humans like order, routine, things going as planned, a box to tick. It helps us feel like we have everything under control. Unfortunately for some, we live in a world that is a hotbed of change, a feast of opinions and stories to tell, and it can make us uneasy and fearful – and sometimes this oozes out of us in a toxic thing called PREJUDICE. And it's the ugliest of ugly when it does.

Hate is a waste; racism a disgrace – and to be influenced by prejudice is cutting yourself off from a world of discovery. We are all flesh and bone, trying to work our way through life – so let's do it together, as one. It will make it all so much less lonely.

If you hear someone voicing hatred or prejudice, even if they are someone close to you, gently challenge why they feel strongly enough to spout negativity. If you experience or witness a hate crime of any sort – this includes physical and/or verbal abuse – it is very important that it is reported to the police.

273

We should all know that racist behaviour is unacceptable. But, while some of us know full well what racism is, others may not realize exactly what defines racism. Here are some things to look out for and guard against doing:

Things that are racist/offensive

Touching people's hair because it's culturally different to yours. I spent a lot of my youth with girls yanking gently and lovingly at my braid extensions. It didn't really anger me or anything; it's nice for people to show an interest. But grabbing people's hair is quite an invasion of space, and kinda makes that person feel a little like a clown!

Assuming someone will act a certain way or do certain things or have a certain mindset because of their religion or the colour of skin. You don't know anyone till you know them – so ask questions to find out what they're about rather than making assumptions.

Using inflammatory racist names. It doesn't matter if you hear other people using them – never use these words.

The following suggestions are provided by twenty-four-year-old Hanna Yusuf:

Casually dropping in comments about the headscarf being a symbol of oppression. I get that in some countries that have oppressive regimes women wear the headscarf, but in liberal countries throughout Europe the headscarf is a part of people's identity. To casually say that it's a symbol of oppression is not just wrong; it's also hugely offensive. How would you like it if something that's part of your identity and that you feel comfortable wearing was labelled as an endorsement of something abhorrent?

274

Conflating cultural practices with the religion of Islam. Female genital mutiliation (FGM) and honour killings are not prescribed by Islam. Some people that carry out those horrible practices happen to be Muslim, but the practitioners aren't exclusively Muslim. It's highly offensive when people don't take the time to learn the facts before making these wrong claims.

Assuming that I'm married or asking about my marital status, as if that is relevant. I don't need a husband to live my life, thank you very much. (This applies to all women of all religions, to be honest.)

Things that aren't racist/offensive

Using the correct term for someone's cultural identity as a way of describing someone in a non-derogatory way, for example, 'She was the tall white girl with ginger hair at the party.'

Asking someone when appropriate and in an inquisitive and kind way about their culture or heritage.

Supporting anti-racial campaigns regardless of your own skin colour or background. In the same way that a man can be a feminist, you don't have to be repressed or attacked yourself to back anti-racism movements.

FEMINISM

IT'S EASY:
YOU ARE A
FEMINIST
IF YOU BELIEVE
IN EQUALITY FOR
MEN AND
WOMEN.

276

A lot of people think it's a little grumpy, but feminism is pretty awesome. It's essentially a powerful belief that we live in a patriarchal society (a society essentially run and governed by men) and that this ain't cool. To be a feminist in the most basic of terms means to believe in equality. Some feminists campaign for it societally, domestically and professionally in a number of ways. Feminists believe that the objectification of women, which has very much been ingrained in us, is damaging, disturbing and undermining. Feminists do not believe that men are evil or that women are better than men. They believe that women are equally as valuable and important in society as men and should be treated as such, and not be valued or judged by their looks – or feel that they have to dress any particular way – or judged by their ability to reproduce, but by their equal contribution to the workplace and beyond. Feminism makes sense. Calling yourself a feminist does not tag you as a man-hater or someone who does not like to be feminine – it tags you as someone who believes in equality. Women can be beautiful and powerful, they can be leaders and carers, they can be loud and wild if they choose or just one or none of those things if they choose. Women are almightily dynamic. Being a feminist means you are a champion of the rights of other women to achieve all that they are capable of. Many men are feminists too.

There is a fascinating and rich tapestry of feminist movements out there, not one size fits all. We all have different reference points and experiences. There so many sections of feminism for this reason. Research them for yourself and enjoy finding out which thread of activism/campaign/literature works for you. Once you start to look, there will be thousands of entry points to a wonderful and fulfilling feminism that appeals to you. I warn you, though, it can be overwhelming. Don't exhaust yourself thinking you are the only warrior having to think about it all, all the time. There isn't enough time in a lifetime to right all the wrongs. Feminism isn't about one person being the saviour, it's about respect and togetherness and fairness. Don't forget to have some fun too.

So, are you a feminist?

YES ☐　NO ☐

If yes, then welcome aboard.

FURTHER READING ON FEMINISM

Girl Up by Laura Bates

How to Be a Woman by Caitlin Moran

What's a Girl Gotta Do? by Holly Bourne

What is Feminism? Why Do We Need It? And Other Big Questions by Bea Appleby and Louise Spilsbury

Bad Feminist by Roxane Gay

My Life on the Road by Gloria Steinem

We Should All Be Feminists by Chimamanda Ngozi Adichie

277

TRAVEL

STOCKHOLM

BERLIN

LONDON

PARIS

ISTANBUL

NEW YORK
TORONTO

ATHENS

MARRAKESH

MEXICO CITY

RIO

CAPE TOWN

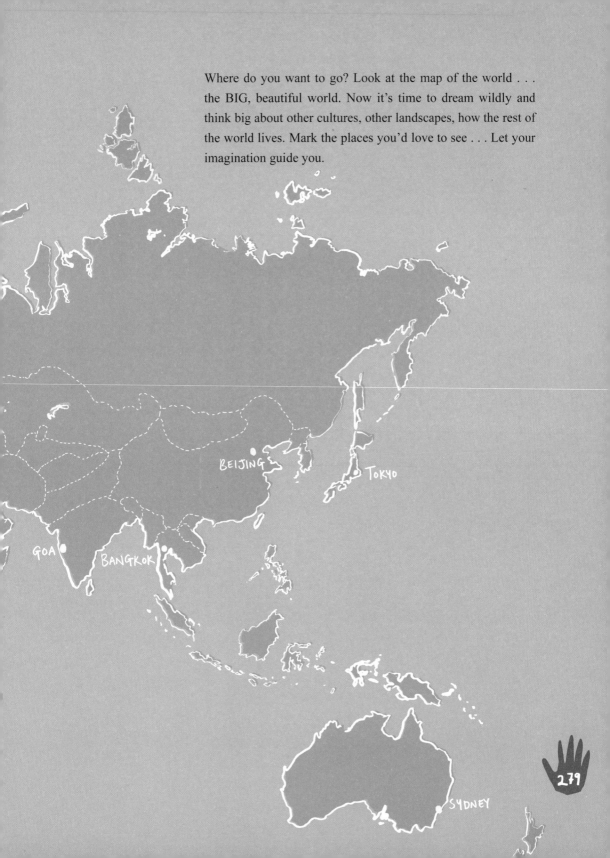

Where do you want to go? Look at the map of the world . . . the BIG, beautiful world. Now it's time to dream wildly and think big about other cultures, other landscapes, how the rest of the world lives. Mark the places you'd love to see . . . Let your imagination guide you.

BEIJING

TOKYO

GOA

BANGKOK

SYDNEY

279

FINDING WHERE YOU BELONG

Travel can mean a permanent move to somewhere. Sometimes your dreams belong in another country. I spoke to **Lucy**, who made the decision at age twenty-two to leave the UK and move to Greece. Lucy thinks she would never have been able to have the quality of life and the happiness she has now if she had stayed in the UK.

I'm Lucy and I'm from Southampton, but I live in Greece with my husband and young son where I co-manage our family's four-star hotel.

When I was twenty-two years old, a mixture of unhappy events, struggling with London life and poor health led me to decide that I needed to make a change in my life. Leaving my family and friends (my second family) was really hard, but I knew it was the right thing for me to do.

My lifestyle is different in every way to what I had imagined when I was growing up: different career, different culture and different people around me in my everyday life. Working in a hotel rather than on the stage was not what I had envisaged when I was practising accepting my Olivier award in the mirror as a twelve-year-old. But other things came into my life that I hadn't realized, expected (or maybe accepted?) would be so important to me. It took me a long time to interpret that as success rather than failure. Learning to grab change (in all its forms) by the balls is probably the key to most of my achievements.

WANDERLUST + EXPRESSION

A STRONG DESIRE TO TRAVEL

I have a rampant sense of wanderlust within me. I am addicted to far-flung places and new worlds within my world. It makes my eyes feel like they could pop out of my head with glee and happiness when I travel. The first day of this year, I woke up on the fringes of the jungle in Costa Rica. Through the netting in the wooden hut we were staying in, I could see the black curly tail of a monkey. Later that day, I spotted a lime-green beaked toucan, many, many feet above me on the top of the trees.

I would never have believed back at the start of my career – which I love and have worked hard at for eight years – that I would one day be in a position to travel so widely. I would never have thought I'd trek Mount Kenya for charity and cycle to Paris in my lifetime. I never knew I would be happy enough with my own company to fly long-haul or eat dinner in restaurants alone – or have the courage to go to Sierra Leone in West Africa after a severe outbreak during the Ebola epidemic.

I spent my teenage years preparing for a life that didn't factor in time for adventure – I'm not sure why. I guess, despite having access to a decent education, I didn't feel that sense of privilege that would allow me to dream of travel. I never felt worthy of some of life's spectacular experiences. I did grow up in a house with a mother who was open to the world. Having gone to an international school herself, my mum learned French at the age of fourteen to communicate with a boy she'd fallen in love with whilst living in Geneva, Switzerland. She then went on to high school in New York City till she was seventeen, after which she moved to Paris, where she lived on a mattress on the floor, and was a nanny to make ends meet. When I was a young child, Mum had friends from different backgrounds, with different strengths, flavours and stories to offer a small and always inquisitive little me.

But Mum's life has had twists and turns. She suffered trauma and mental-health battles too, and by the time I was teenager, that, along with my own monstrous experiences, had turned the fun into a struggle. And so, when I left home aged eighteen, I was a young person with a conflicted tangle of expectations for my own life. I'd grown up with the tools of expressive communication, and a soul fuelled by energy for experience, and yet I subconsciously prepared for life to be tough.

It wasn't just what I'd seen at home, either. I was in a world where women have to fight harder to gain the confidence to say what they want, to feel like they can be brave enough for ferocious adventure. In a world where it is rare to see darker skin tones than all shades of white represented as 'explorers' of the globe, I am immensely proud and thankful to have done the things I've done so far. To love the world as I do, and be able to take the plunge to go out and discover it . . . it feels like a gift to myself – one that I couldn't recommend more.

So, go to places; ignite your wanderlust! You don't need to go far – organize camping trips with friends, look upwards at the sky and enjoy the magic of clouds, play in the park and roll down hills always. Keep your imagination active; it'll protect you in the most confusing times. And, if you imagine and work hard enough, sometimes some of those dreams will come true. Love the real world and all it has to offer. The amount there is out there to experience and learn from is endless.

MAKE RAINBOWS...

Anyone who knows me knows I am in love with colour. I strongly believe in its power to cheer and heal. So much so that, a few years ago in London, I conducted a social experiment for a brand to brighten people's day.

My task was simply to spark the imaginations of those in the city, any way I saw fit. So between 6 a.m. and 10 a.m. on a Monday morning, I literally turned London Bridge into a rainbow. I specifically chose that day and those hours when life can be particularly challenging, when the relentless morning commute is enough to smash good vibes to smithereens, to make the happiest of people feel like they're having the colour bashed out of them.

The longest rainbow carpet I'll ever see in my life was rolled out across London Bridge, me situated at one end, in a matching rainbow jacket, giving passers-by a single flower each as they walked to work through a jaunty arch that said LOVE MONDAYS.

I'm sounding like a madwoman now, right? Here's the picture to prove it. I find myself again and again having to look at the pictures to believe it too.

What I found was that, although some people were suspicious, ninety per cent of faces broke into a smile . . . and it felt euphoric. A collective euphoria via colour! I watched anyone with their head down walk the full bridge and become dazzled by the rainbow beneath them. I will never forget that day. I got so many hugs. I noticed most people wore hues of brown, black and grey, their sartorial aesthetic blurring into the miserable weather around them.

As the opportunity to roll carpets as big as the BFG's feet is rare, think of alternative ways you can introduce colour and sparkle into your life. You can wear all the colours of the Northern Lights on your body. You can shimmer in sequins that shine as much as the sea on holiday. Fill your bedroom with vases of fire-coloured dahlias to make you smile. There is much power in the brightness of flowers.

AND DANCE. NEVER FORGET TO TURN MUSIC UP LOUD AND BOOGIE.

What would you do to spark your city/town/village community? Write/draw it below.

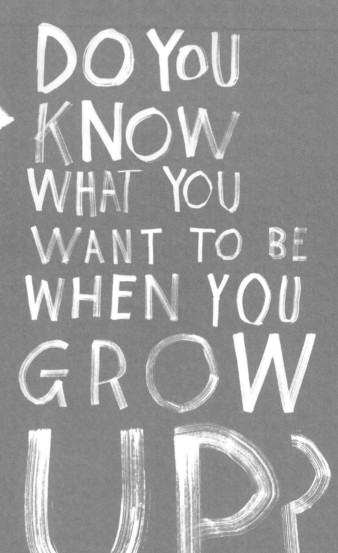

DO YOU KNOW WHAT YOU WANT TO BE WHEN YOU GROW UP?

I ASK YOU THIS, REGARDLESS OF YOUR AGE . . .

286

Allow me to let you into a little secret: hardly anyone knows for sure. Also, this whole 'growing up' thing is a bit of a myth. We may stop physically growing 'up', but we are always adding layers of experience, twisting and turning about the place, forming opinions, fusing, changing and emotionally growing.

So release yourself from the pressure of an 'algorithmic' ideal. Not everything happens in an efficient, prescribed sequence. Success isn't pinned on one exam paper, or on one interview . . . There isn't ONE straight route to anywhere or anything. The paths we must take are complicated, more like those of a maze, with choices to make in every direction and the occasional dead end – so don't be upset with yourself if you're unsure about where you're going, or exactly what will make you happiest. Just follow your instincts, use your imagination, use your brain and use every resource at your disposal.

TRY things. Lots of things. Meet people you admire and aspire to be like for tea. Talk about your maddest of madcap ideas. Collaborate with your peers – whether it's organizing a fundraising event, or setting up a blog. Exchanging thoughts and ideas – even if it's just to make each other laugh, and laugh, and laugh – is stimulating. It will get you thinking. Sparks will fly. You don't have to project too far ahead or rush headlong into your newfound goal or ideal . . . Savour every moment of learning; relish every challenge.

I want to pierce through the belief that success at school, or not messing up an internship, is the be-all and end-all. Everybody makes mistakes – think of them of as experiences, and learn from them. Do your best; try to be kind; work hard and relax. Weirdly, when you are relaxed you are usually the most confident – you are expressive and true, and therefore you will do your best. If you don't get the grade you wanted, or you don't get that job, you're not going to die. There will be a way, an alternative – and everything is going to be OK. So don't believe the hype that everything rests on one thing going right.

Mentors & * * Role Models

Role model: *a person looked up to by others as an example to follow.*

Role models and mentors are invaluable. You are never too young or too old to have one. Of the things I'm most humbly grateful for in my life, all the generous-spirited people I have learned from are right up there at the top – whether it's those I call friends or those that I've taken the time to seek out, listen to and study. It's rewarding and important to spend time on researching incredible people of the past and present who embody a healthy and compassionate philosophy, message or energy that you can connect to in some way. It doesn't mean you should necessarily aspire to become them exactly – but educating yourself about aspirational figures is good for you.

Grace Jones

Erykah Badu

Spice Girls

The Slits

We are lucky to live in a time when we have access and exposure to a wealth of arts, cultures and subcultures so diverse they are a firework of fun to learn about and become inspired by. There are some incredible women, for example, who have offered sparks of irreverence that have inspired me over the years, and been awesome in helping me feel like it's OK to be me.

Who do you see that makes you feel excited to be you? Fill in the blanks with your own role-model firework.

Mentor: *an experienced and trusted adviser.*

A mentor in your life can enhance it greatly. There is a brilliant list of organizations at the back of the book that offer mentorship schemes of different types.

I mentor brilliant **June Eric-Udorie**. She is a writer and so impressively clever. She is eight years younger than me. We meet for a hot chocolate every few months and talk about what we're up to. For me, mentoring June has shown me how hard it is to be young right now, and how so many young people are inspiringly unselfish – they are, in fact, supremely advanced thinkers who want a better society for all. They are less reckless than I was at that age, more thoughtful. I want to let June know just how awesome she is. In return, she gave me some amazing advice when I first told her about this book. She sent me many awesome reading lists and pieces written by the best writers on the subject of writing. June knows SO much, and I learn from her every time we hang out.

Talking to June Eric-Udorie

GC: What do you get out of having a mentor?

JE-U: There are lots of benefits to having a mentor — someone who can guide you with decisions [about] your career or just life in general . . . They provide insight, push you to think differently, and help remind you of your value and worth. But I think the best thing about having [Gem] as a mentor is just being able to learn from her. I watch as my mentor takes up space and is brave and fun and jolly and smart, and the ways in which she practises the lessons that she's trying to teach me. It's heart-warming, knowing there's someone you can always reach out to, but it's even better having a mentor that embodies the sort of person you want to be. You can look up to her when you're not feeling as motivated or courageous. I find myself thinking, 'What would Gemma do?'

GC: Do you mentor anyone?

JE-U: I do a little bit of academic mentoring with Integrate, a Bristol-based charity that works primarily with black, minority, ethnic and refugee kids in the UK. I really enjoy it, but in the future I'd really like to mentor black girls and young women, because I think it's so important that they have cheerleaders and supporters and people who are on their side, especially when we live in a world where we are still, very much, relegated to the shadows.

My mentor is a badass of a woman called Karen Blackett. She's witty, smart and graciously brave, and is the CEO of one of the UK's most influential media companies. Karen advises on and creates content for some of the UK's biggest advertising campaigns. She also has a fabulous glass office, with lovely photographs everywhere, and everyone around her respects her immensely.

Talking to Karen Blackett, OBE

GC: What do you get out of being a mentor?

KB: By mentoring someone else, it actually leads to reverse-mentoring. I get to draw on my experience to help someone else, but I also learn and challenge my brain. The gift of helping others is a blessing. Seeing someone else progress and achieve is a massive reward. I genuinely believe with the right support and guidance, determination and resilience, work ethic and focus, anyone can achieve their goals. We have it within us to make our dreams, however big or small, a reality.

GC: Who is your mentor?

KB: Lawyer, businesswoman and broadcaster Dame Heather Rabbatts.

Talking to Dame Heather Rabbatts

GC: What do you get out of being a mentor?

DHR: I think what I get out of being a mentor is always learning. Mentoring is two-way . . . in trying to offer insight to others, you inevitably reflect on your own experiences and different perspectives evolve. I totally value the development for both the mentee and myself, and know it enriches my life.

I have never had a mentor as such but for me my group of women friends have always been there and offered great guidance and support — so I have been truly blessed!

292

MONEY
MONEY
MONEY

...AKA: CASHOLA, SPONDULAS, WONGA, NOTES, DOLLAR DOLLAR BILL, Y'ALL.

I have expensive ta$te

Money = a scramble. Either a scramble to get it, or a scramble to use it wisely if you have some. We all need money to live, and it's great to have a bit extra – to go out, go on holidays, buy nice things. But money can mess you up too. If you don't have enough, it is miserable: it can lead to health problems; it's tough on friendships; it can make you despair. If you have too much, it can set you apart from friends; it doesn't make you a better person; it doesn't stop you feeling lonely . . . It doesn't solve your problems.

Life is like a game of Monopoly, involving luck, decisions and moral choices. Whatever your money situation – the main thing is to be in control of your finances. Don't let money control you – don't become obsessed with it. Do develop healthy attitudes to money early on. Learn to live within your means. Clue yourself up about saving and what different kinds of bank accounts entail and mean for you. We don't get taught about the practicalities of money at school, which is bizarre, as it is so pivotal to security and stability – even our health. So it's up to YOU to get smart.

294

I spoke to an awesome charity called My Bnk, which believes money should be a subject on the curriculum. My Bnk visits schools, colleges and universities to explain some of the hard-to-understand basics.

Drink it up: some of these words could save ya some money.

As a nation, we can be obsessed with money. For different reasons, though. For some, it comes from a place of goodwill — they are obsessed with the bigger picture, like setting up their own business and striving to make a success of it. Some let money govern them unhealthily; others think about it a lot, and it affects their emotional well-being because they don't have enough. Our attitude to credit is changing. Older generations were much more credit-loving, which led to a lot of people in deep debt. That's changing, and we're collectively getting more savvy to how that can go wrong.

M⊙NEY
KEY TERMS AND TOP TIPS

The key things to remember are **simple**, really.

Credit is borrowed money. When you have a credit card, you are borrowing money, which, if you don't pay it back within a certain time period, you are charged interest on. This interest is different depending on who you borrow the money from. But essentially it means you're going to have to pay back more than you borrowed in the first place. Credit cards aren't bad things if you use them wisely; they can help with emergencies, for example. As long as you know that it isn't your money and that you must pay it back as soon as possible.

When considering a credit card for the first time, it's important to not get reeled in by the 'glamour' aspect of 'plastic'. It can feel so much better to pay for things with your own hard-earned cash.

Payday lenders. There are lots of different angles to these, but, essentially, they work on a similar premise to credit. They make money by charging high interest rates on the cash they lend you.

Debt is money you owe.

Incorporating an income timeline. It's never too early think about an income timeline. Making sure your income and outgoings line up now will help when you are managing your finances as an adult. If you have learned **budgeting** and **saving** skills before you're eighteen, then you're less likely to need to borrow money – and, if you *do* borrow it, you're going to understand why you're borrowing it, and it'll be structured.

Inform yourself as a consumer. Where's your money going? Know that you've essentially got control.

Types of accounts. There are enough to bamboozle even the smartest of folk out there. Remember this and do your research. There are **current accounts** and **savings accounts** – that's as complicated as it should really get. But they're all called different things: a **flex account**, a **gold account**, a **platinum account** – they've all got different names according to different banks. **Compare the AER (annual equivalent rate)** on accounts if you want to be a **saver**. If you're looking at **borrowing**, then you need to **compare the APR (annual percentage rate)**. It's so refreshing to have the tools to find what you want in a bank account. So look up the small print and ask questions when you're in the bank.

Overdrafts. These are super common because they're seen as a 'safety net'. Often people start with them at university, when they're interest free. They are helpful if you need a little extra money at the end of the month; but, as with other forms of credit, they do need to be paid back.

University. At the moment, a three-year university course will cost around **£50,000**, which covers **tuition fees** and a **maintenance loan**. It's important not to focus too heavily on the 'owing' and think about the benefits of **learning and experience** that you get from university, as it's all too easy to become overwhelmed. If you do decide to go, remember that it's important to plan in advance how you are going to **budget** your money whilst there. Also remember that you don't have to start paying these loans back until you're earning over a certain salary threshold after you have graduated.

297

If you have a **dream**, be **passionate** and **source** the right help. There are loads of **cool organizations** out there that **support young people's businesses** – that will help you get **grants** and get **funding**. You just have to have a **good idea**, engage a **strong sense of identity** and **focus**. Be **confident, positive**, know your market, do your **research**. Ask yourself – **has anything been done like this before?** Have you tried and **tested it** – or has someone else tested it, and it flopped? Why did it flop? Learn from their mistakes and be patient.

Tax. Don't forget it. You'll pay income tax on income above your Personal Allowance.

Know your tax status, and how you're paying yours – whether you are saving it each month if you're self-employed, or if it is deducted at source by your employer.

DON'T PANIC!

THERE ARE LOTS OF PEOPLE YOU CAN ASK FOR ADVICE . . . and there is a list of organizations that can help you at the back of this book.

Great money-management apps are:

Toshl Finance – a spending app that helps track your outgoings.

OnTrees – all your bank accounts on one platform.

ClearScore – free credit score and report on your phone.

BUDGET PLANNER

INCOME

Saturday or part-time job

Parental allowance

(Occasionally selling stuff on eBay)

OUTGOINGS

Clothes/sports stuff

Beauty products

Phone bill

Music/TV/games downloads/books or DVDs

Hobbies

Cinema

Meals out

Snacks/drinks

Tampons and other life essentials

OCCASIONAL COSTS

Birthday or Christmas gifts

Long-distance travel

Holidays

Gigs/festivals/events

Hair – cut or colour

Nail bar/other beauty treatments

Gadgets/computer

Budget planner by My Bnk

299

CAREERS

I believe you can be anything you want to be in this world. Anyone can be. I truly believe it. You don't have to be what your mum or dad wishes, what a 'career advisor' advises or even what you thought you might be at a different point in your life. The clichés are true: if you work hard enough, your dreams can come true. I believe that because mine did, and more. Your dreams change, too, as you grow. That's part of the fun.

The hula hooper

What you personally want to be in life might jump outside convention and bend others' minds. I interviewed one such irreverent, imaginative, gutsy, hard-grafting woman: the global bend machine that is *Marawa The Amazing*. Marawa is a world-record-holding professional hula hooper and is toppest of top in the hula hooping game.

GC: How does one end up being a professional hula hooper? Is it something that you always wanted to do?

M: No, not at all . . . I think it could've easily been something else. I really didn't know, going into it, what I was doing. The key thing was that I studied a Bachelor of Circus Arts degree, and ended up getting into the circus. It was a brand-new degree, and I thought that it sounded really interesting. I didn't know where it was going to lead; I didn't know it was going to lead to being a professional hula hooper! I did gymnastics in high school. I really liked arty stuff, but was encouraged to follow an academic route, and I did two years of social science and creative writing at university. I really liked sociology, and I really liked writing, but I wasn't convinced that it was the course for me, and I didn't know what I would do for a job at the end of it.

Then in my early/mid-twenties I got into the circus school, and I was like, 'Right then, let's give this a go!' And ever since then I've felt like I was not *getting away with it*, but I felt like I was on holiday all the time. I was turning up in a tracksuit every day, and my job was to climb up some ropes and work on my flexibility, which felt like the best thing ever. It felt like a holiday. Then getting into shows, and doing shows, I was like, 'This is not work. This is the best fun ever — literally.'

GC: How did you translate going to circus school into a career and business and being able to travel the world?

M: I was really lucky. I get paid enough that I can do the things I want to do and save a bit too. And I've chosen a skill that I can keep doing until I'm seventy-five.

301

GC: Tell me about the troupe.

M: That was a project with the Roundhouse where they asked me to choreograph a group to do a group hoop performance for the Olympic torch relay. We did the project and it worked really well. We had twelve girls, and I taught them. Some of them weren't hoopers at all — they just wanted to be in it. So we taught them how to hoop, and put the routine together . . . Now I can step back a little bit and train up the next generation of hoopers.

GC: What does your dad now think of your job?

M: I'd managed to get away with not telling him until I was thirty. He thought I'd finished my social science degree, and then he wasn't really sure what I was doing. He likes to Skype with me every now and then just to remind me that I might want to come home and finish my studies and get serious again.

GC: What are your top tips about travel?

M: Shelter, food, safety. That's it. Book your flight, book a cheap hostel — do your research, find a reputable place to stay. You can go anywhere in the world. Just leave the hotel and just walk. I'll just walk and walk and walk, and try and keep it relatively simple so you don't need a map. That's how I think you really get a taste for a place.

How amazing is it to have a career out of making people laugh? Being a comedian is an ACTUAL job. I talked to the awesome, smart and funny *Aisling Bea* about how to get into the world of 'comedy'.

Aisling's advice

Start in your sitting room entertaining your cat, and upgrade to your friends, then strangers. Practise speaking your bits out loud. Record yourself, on paper and on your phone. Start bringing a notebook with you everywhere and jot down things that happen. For stand-up, get stage time, hop on everywhere, start your own gigs if there are none, hone your craft, throw yourself into it and make a community of fellow artists so you can all help bring each other up. Talk to everyone. Don't ask everyone for their opinion, only people you trust. And TRY and enjoy it — you are aiming to make people a bit happier. Stay focused on that. Wear shoes you feel make you confident so you can plant your feet properly. YOU GOT THIS.

It is not hard to get into comedy — what is tough is STAYING in comedy. When you have a bad gig, or someone is mean, or you feel that cringe of silence and don't want to ever see people again, or when you don't make money and have to trek around and sleep on couches, or if you get writer's block, that is hard. That is when you have to dig down and remember that you ARE funny.

The scientist

Dr Selina Wray is a senior research associate at UCL Institute of Neurology. She is pioneering development in the treatment of dementia.

Selina's advice

I'm very lucky to work in a really diverse group — male, female, from all different backgrounds, all different nationalities — which is one of the things that I love about my job: getting to interact with people from across many different cultures . . . just all really enthusiastic about the science. My boss and head of department really believe that it doesn't matter where you come from in terms of background, ethnicity or anything — if you've got a passion for the science and you enjoy doing the science, you're welcome.

The footballer

Girls kick ass at football. It is a brilliant career choice, and not just something you see when the Olympics is on TV. I spoke to Danielle Carter, who is twenty-three and a professional footballer. Danielle's proudest moment is scoring a hat-trick on her Senior England debut in the Lionesses.

Danielle's advice

Be prepared to sacrifice your time. There will be times where you won't be able to attend certain events with friends, for example, as you'll have to prioritize your preparation for games/training. Once you finally get your breakthrough, continue to work as hard as you did, if not harder, to make sure you are the best you can be. And don't fall short or become complacent and get left behind!

Finally . . . ENJOY! Enjoy what you do and embrace your journey. Everyone's path in life is different; don't compare yours to anyone else . . . Be patient, work hard and keep the faith.

TREADING ON YOUR OWN PATH

We've talked about the possibilities for your professional path and the importance of following your gut, your passion and thinking 'outside the box'. Life is not a neat form with little tick boxes that you check off. It doesn't work like that.

My advice? Spend time on yourself, get some experiences under your belt, challenge yourself with new things, explore your potential as far as you can and don't let what your peers are doing, or a newspaper headline, throw you off course. Chances are that once you are happy and secure in yourself and what you are doing, the other stuff will fall into place. But the most important thing to remember is that you don't have to have what everyone else has, or even want it, to be a valuable human being. You are amazing – just the way you are.

Me? I have had the dream job and realize that the dream always changes and I will never tire of new challenges. I got an A in my English GCSE and an E in Maths, and I didn't go to university. I am yet to have children and have no idea what will happen when I choose to do that. I have never been married. But, above all, I love deeply. That is the single most important thing to remember on your path. TO LOVE.

NOW GO REACH FOR THE MOOON!

A LETTER TO MYSELF AGED 14

Dear Me

You don't have to rush. There is plenty of time to feel all the feelings there are to be felt. You will feel them all and, when you do, they will be huge. Though they will never stop being confusing, there is no light-bulb moment when it'll all make sense, no age between now and thirty-one where you will understand everything life throws at you. Your feelings will always change, just like your hair will. I know you think about these things every night before you go to sleep, but there is so much time for dancing, sparkly clothes, kissing and electric body tingles, so just wait a bit longer before you actually do them.

Keep letting the ridiculous ideas that flood your brain flow about like a song storm inside you. They are part of who you are and they will never stop. Remember when you were nine and you circled all the publishers in the 'P' section of the yellow pages, because you were gonna contact them to publish your book? You will write it one day.

Your boobs will get bigger too. So stop trying to think of ways you can make them bigger; stop researching those lie-herbal pills that promise to 'naturally enhance your bust' – it's a load of shit. A TOTAL load of shit. They will not enhance any bust. You will cringe so hard at the fact that you used to cross the straps of your padded bra at the back, squeezing your AA cups together to create the strangest-looking tiny cleavage. Quit whilst you're ahead. Oh, and you don't need to wear foundation, honestly you don't. Your skin is amazing, even with those spots on your forehead. The limited choice of foundation shades you can get in your town are completely wrong for you and, if I'm honest, make your face look like it's been smeared in a light dusting of chalk. By the way, the spots will disappear and the scars don't even stay, so stop hating your face.

The rest of you will get bigger too, but never focus too hard on how much. Your body will change with the times, as will your brain. It will adapt to the world around you, which'll be a fun one, I promise. Your body will be loved and treated with tender loving care by others, so try to learn to do the same. Exhaust yourself by playing and exploring, you don't need to think about exercise, just keep thrashing about. Drink loads of water, like at any given opportunity, guzzle, guzzle, gulp, glug it.

Never be ashamed of who you are. Sometimes you are, as they say, 'a bit much', 'too loud' and 'quite annoying', but who gives a f*ck? Especially as the good people in your life will like you that way. You can live your own story and it doesn't have to be anybody else's. Listen to your gut, it makes even better decisions than your brain or your heart does sometimes.

You don't have to be like anyone else: no celebrity, prefect at your school or anyone else you've come across or know. Listen to your weirdness – it comes from having a gigantic imagination and boundless hope. It will always help you to appreciate colour, travel, nature and many types of people. There are extraordinary people everywhere on this planet, so even when you think the world is too awful to bear, trust in your love of exploring, talking, dancing and staring at vast open spaces and the twinkling sea – it'll see you through and keep your perspective fresh. Be proud of your ability to love your friends, but beware of the toxic ones.

Keep loving new opportunities and new ways of experiencing things. You don't have a 'bad attitude', like some of the teachers say you do. Try to learn to channel the energy and the incessant question-asking into learning rather than bedazzling mischief. You will always love to be mischievous, but will learn that the best way is to mix it with good – it's still *well* fun, but feels better peppered with a little sophistication and creativity. Being plain bad is boring and guilt-ridden.

Keep reading, keep writing. Keep asking the big, hard questions about things that don't feel right in life, things that are unjust. But you don't have to scream them, even if the truth makes you rage and your face hot. You don't always know what's right, no one single person does. You have more power than you think. Engage in politics and keep absorbing history with the inquisitive, spongy nature you have. You are far from stupid even though you will always be catastrophic at maths. You will never know what you want to be when you grow up, and will realize that most people don't.

You're going to be all right. There isn't as much struggle as you subconsciously prepare for.

Ask for help, rather than getting angry. Anger rusts a person's morals and clouds vision, it doesn't suit you, so breathe deep – you will learn to be happy and you are not a bad person. Bad is a bad word, to apply to yourself only if you are dancing to a Michael Jackson song or using the term 'badass'.

You don't have to give in emotionally to a love that feels out of control. You are strong and you have more control than you think. You have time to run to where it is safer. You *can* get out of this. If the love feels bad and unhealthy, if it makes you mostly sad, it isn't a good love. There are others out there, willing to give you a good love, so break up with the boy who is hurting you. Honestly, I know you can't imagine it, but get out of it now. It'll be so much better for you in the end if you do.

Keep your mind open. Don't judge others or abide by the constraints of the imposed class system or stereotyping. Don't forget, no one is too special or not good enough to communicate with. You will learn something from nearly everyone you meet.

Please stop shaving your bikini line, the shaving-rash marks will remain forever.

Be you and keep your head held high.

Love Gem
Aged 31

THANK YOU!

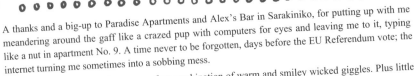

AISLING BEA > PAGE 303
© KARLA GOWLETT

AURELIA LANGE >
ILLUSTRATOR

KAREN BLACKETT
OBE > PAGE 292

LAURA CAIRNEY-KEIZE >
PAGE 155

JOSIE LONG >
PAGE 232

ANNA HART >
PAGE 154

AMY REDMOND >
PAGE 155

LITERARY AGENT >
BECKY THOMAS

IZZY > PAGE 264

JANENE SPENCER >
DESIGNER

BRIGITTE APHRODITE >
PAGES 19 + 154
© OLIVIER RICHOMME

GEORGIE OKELL > PAGE 183
© JON LAWTON

RACHEL VALE >
ART DIRECTOR

FRANCES ACQUAAH >
PAGES 52 + 155

A thanks and a big-up to Paradise Apartments and Alex's Bar in Sarakiniko, for putting up with me meandering around the gaff like a crazed pup with computers for eyes and leaving me to it, typing like a nut in apartment No. 9. A time never to be forgotten, days before the EU Referendum vote; the internet turning me sometimes into a sobbing mess.

Thank you, Mrs Dragon, for your perfect combination of warm and smiley wicked giggles. Plus little Riko too, for merely providing the brilliance and innocence of a baby genius who loves the sea even more than I do.

Thank you to Sara Jane at the Coach House, for providing the perfect solitary escape.

Thank you, Jim, I love you – I have been a NIGHTMARE. 2016: nightmare girlfriend – you survived it!

Thank you, Becky Thomas, for listening to my hare-brained idea, when I collared you in a stinky pub. Thank you, Rachel P and Gaby, for reining me in. Thank you, Emily, for being my carer. Thank you, Rachel V, for not writing swear words back when I was being so clueless and yet bossy in my emails. Thank you, Kat, for sharing the wheels-on-the-bus-going-round-and-round vision from the get-go. Thank you to Bea, for your lovely energy of enthusiasm and care for this project! Thank you to all of team Open. YOU are AMAZING.

Thank you, Aurelia. WOW you have blown us away. Anyone who takes a manic message about a smiling condom and makes it into an iconic picture is frankly magnificent.

Thank you, SJ, for being the slickest and most resilient life cheerleader always.

Thank you, Woo, for ALWAYS feeding and challenging my brain, and for listening to me relentlessly wang ON.

Thank you, BriGaz, you are a treasure to know – and give endless inspiration and love.

Thank you to ALL ma crew. My friends for always nodding when I'm chatting tripe, scooping me up when I go crazy, never making me feel judged or misunderstood, for being the BEST FUN. YEP, that's you, brother from another mother and deep inspiration Laurence (aka Lozini); you, my forever bestie Camilla (CamCam); Scott (Scottie-too-hottie); beautiful and kind Sarah (Baker), Sam (aka monsieur le mayor) and your new addition baby Bow; Dallanda (aka Trojan), gorgeous Niklas and your magic Baby Issaga; determined and brilliant Claudia (Cloudini) and Matt (Clark Kent), thank you for always supporting me in the *Birmingham Mail*. Thank you, Amy (Zing), for being as warm and colourful as a walking rainbow and introducing me to a home town I could find the calm to write a book in.

Thank you to Katie V, for trawling through lots of gabbing.

Thanks, Amber and Rob, for not batting an eyelid when I was a sweaty monster furiously typing in my room and regurgitating angst during the process.

Thank you, to the boyz, the loves of the past mentioned in *Open*, for you have taught me all I am and how to love, heal and love again. Thank you, Mr Smith.

Thank you to Becky and Daniella, the most patient and talented videographers in the country.

Thank you, Nash and Dockers, for being gifted, wordy dreamers and for making feel like I could be the same.

Thank you to all those at the Beeb, who trained me up good and proper, and believed in me to give the opportunities that you have.

Thank you to those in my industry who I count as dear and supportive friends and mad-core inspirationals – that's you, Lala & Dawn.

Thank you to Mum, Laura and Daddy Cool for continuously putting up with me.

AND OF COURSE ALL THE CONTRIBUTORSSSSS . . . You were too ace for me not to include you in this book.

JESSICA JORDAN-WRENCH > PAGE 154
© KIM CONWAY

DAN GLASER >
PAGES 61 + 98
DAME HEATHER RABBATTS
> PAGE 292

ASHLEY FULWOOD > PAGE 89

JUNO DAWSON > PAGE 189 © JOEL RYDER

ZEZI IFORE > PAGE 154

DR ALISON ATTRILL-SMITH > PAGE 253

HANNA YUSUF > PAGE 274 © ELYAS SONIUS

GEORGE LESTER >
EDITORIAL ASSISTANT

GEORGIA LEWIS-ANDERSON
> PAGE 155

LAURA DARRALL > PAGE 78

LUCY > PAGE 280

DR RADHA > PAGE 145

CAROLINE ROTHSTEIN > PAGE 86
© CHRISTOPHER CLAUSS

JESSICA THANDI
BERRY > PAGE 155

KAT MCKENNA >
MARKETING MANAGER

LIV GAL-DEM > PAGE 262

SOPHIE AND OSCAR > PAGE 13

MARAWA CAMARA >
PAGE 300

DR CAROLINE TAYLOR
> PAGE 70

LAUREN > PAGE 13

NIC ADDISON > PAGE 170

EMMA GIBSON > PAGE 154
© GABRIELLE HALL

MICHAEL > PAGE 13

UNE ERIC-UDORIE > PAGE 291

JO SWINSON > PAGE 231

EMILY THOMAS > EDITOR

DR SELINA WRAY > PAGE 304

ANONYMOUS SELF-HARMER > PAGE 104

LEO PEMBERTON >
PAGE 85

EDITORIAL DIRECTOR
NON-FICTION & POETRY
> GABY MORGAN

SURAN D AND SONNY > PAGE 186

DANIELLE CARTER > PAGE 304

ROSE BRETÉCHER > PAGE 90

BEA CROSS >
PUBLICITY MANAGER

PROF HUGH MONTGOMERY
> PAGE 127

KAREN ROBINSON >
PAGE 270

KELLY ABBOT > PAGE 200

BEEKEEPER BECCA > PAGE 242

ANONYMOUS
INTERVIEW >
PAGE 216

RACHEL PETTY > EDITORIAL
DIRECTOR

KATIE V > TRANSCRIBING WHIZZ

SUSIE ORBACH > PAGE 84

USEFUL WEBSITES

YOUR HEART

Abusive Relationships
www.lovedontfeelbad.co.uk
www.womensaid.org.uk

Emotional and Physical Abuse (Teens)
www.childline.org.uk
www.nspcc.org.uk

Bullying
www.ditchthelabel.org
www.bulliesout.com
www.kidscape.org.uk
www.antibullyingpro.com

Loneliness
www.mind.org.uk/Loneliness

Bereavement
www.winstonswish.org.uk
www.rainbowtrust.org.uk
www.muchloved.com
www.cruse.org.uk

YOUR MIND

www.sane.org.uk
www.mind.org.uk

Counselling/Psychotherapy
www.icap.org.uk
www.bacp.co.uk
www.counsellingfoundation.org

Depression
www.mind.org.uk/information-support/types-
   of-mental-health-problems/depression
www.pandasfoundation.org.uk
www.rethink.org/diagnosis-treatment/
   conditions/depression

Suicide Charities
www.samaritans.org.uk
www.allianceofhope.org
www.maytree.org.uk

Eating Disorders
www.anorexiabulimiacare.org.uk
www.b-eat.co.uk
www.seedeatingdisorders.org.uk

OCD
www.ocduk.org
www.ocdaction.org.uk

Addiction
www.actiononaddiction.org.uk
www.addaction.org.uk
www.lighthousefoundation.org.uk

Self-Harm
www.selfharm.co.uk
www.selfinjurysupport.org.uk

YOUR BODY AND SOUL

Body Image
www.bodycharity.co.uk
www.berealcampaign.co.uk
www.bodygossip.org

Periods
www.periodpositive.com

Rape and Sexual Offences
content.met.police.uk/Site/sapphire
www.mybodybackproject.com
www.rapecrisis.org.uk
www.thesurvivorstrust.org

Asexuality
www.whatisasexuality.com

LGBTQ Charities
www.akt.org.uk
www.stonewall.org.uk
www.glaad.org
www.itgetsbetter.org

Transgender Charities/Organizations
www.genderedintelligence.co.uk
www.mermaidsuk.org.uk

Sexual Health
whenitsonitson.durex.co.uk
www.brook.org.uk
www.fpa.org.uk

Abortion
www.bpas.org
www.mariestopes.org.uk
www.nupas.co.uk

Porn
www.porn-recovery.co.uk
www.cosrt.org.uk
www.sexaddictionhelp.co.uk
www.atsac.co.uk

YOUR WORLD AND YOUR FUTURE

Politics
www.globalissues.org
www.theyworkforyou.com

The Planet
www.greenpeace.org.uk
Mentoring & Volunteering
www.arts-emergency.org
www.megaphonewrite.com
www.womentoringproject.co.uk
www.princes-trust.org.uk
www.timebank.org.uk/

The Internet
www.bbc.co.uk/webwise
www.revengepornhelpline.org.uk

Online Magazines
www.gal-dem.com
www.thatswhatss.com

Missing People
www.missingpeople.org.uk

INDEX